FORTY-?

YEARS

A CIVIL SERVANT

FORTY-THREE
YEARS
A CIVIL SERVANT

With references to my schooldays and previous employment

ROYSTON J TUCKER

BROWN
DOG
BOOKS

Published under licence by Brown Dog Books and
The Self-Publishing Partnership, 7 Green Park Station,
Bath BA1 1JB

www.selfpublishingpartnership.co.uk

ISBN printed book: 978-1-83952-029-7
ISBN e-book: 978-1-83952-030-3

Cover design by Kevin Rylands
Internal design by Andrew Easton

Hansard cover image reproduced by kind permission of the Parliamentary Archives. Photo of the shop floor reproduced by kind permission of the Weir Group; photos of steel-making process and guide reproduced by kind permission of British Steel Corporation; photo of stud link chain cable reproduced by kind permission of Griffin Woodhouse.

This book is printed on FSC certified paper

Printed and bound in Great Britain by
CPI Group (UK) Ltd, Croydon CR0 4YY

TABLE OF CONTENTS

ABBREVIATIONS

A
ADMATS   Admiralty Materials
AEW   Admiralty Experimental Works
AFC   Associated Football Club
AFO   Admiralty Fleet Order
ASI   Ascension Island
AUWE   Admiralty Underwater Weapons Establishment
AWO   Admiralty Welfare Officer

B
BATSUB   British Army Training Support Unit Belize
BR   Book of Reference
BRNC   Britannia Royal Naval College

C
CA   Civil Assistant
CAD   Computer Aided Design
CB   Classified Book
CC   Cubic Capacity
CCFRA   Chipping Camden Food Research Association
CDR   Commander
CE II   Civilian Establishments Branch Two
CED   Chief Executive, Dockyards
CEO   Chief Executive Officer
CINO   Chief Inspector Naval Ordnance

CivSec/FI	Civil Secretary/Falkland Islands
CO	Clerical Officer
C of E	Church of England
C of N	Controller of the Navy
CS	Civil Service
CSCA	Civil Service Clerical Association
CVA.01	Cancelled Replacement Aircraft Carrier

D	
DCG	Defence Catering Group
DCI	Defence Council Instructions
DEng	Director Engineering
DEE	Director on Electrical Engineering
DFM	Directorate of Food Supply
DG	Director General
DGShips	Director General Ships
DGW(N)	Director General Weapons(Navy)
DGD&M	Director General Dockyards & Maintenance
DME	Director of Mechanical Engineering
DMS(N)	Director of Marine Services(Naval)
DNC	Director of Naval Construction
DNE	Director Naval Equipment
DNEE	Director of Naval of Electrical Engineering
DGNPS	Director General Naval Personnel Services
DNSP	Director Naval Ship Production
DRP(S)	Director Resources and Programmes (Ships)
DSFM	Directorate of Services Food Management
D&B	Dun and Bradstreet
DWD	Director of Warship Design

E	
EO	Executive Officer

EU/OJ	European Union/Official Journal
F	
FCO	Foreign and Commonwealth Office
FRICS	Fellow Royal Institute Chartered Surveyors
G	
GCE	General Certificate of Education
GCHQ	Government Communications Headquarters
GO-GO	Government Owned Government Operated
GO-CO	Government Owned Contractor Operated
H	
HEO	Higher Executive Officer
HM	Her Majesty's
HMD	Her Majesty's Dockyard
HMNB	Her Majesty's Naval Base
HMS	Her Majesty's Ship
HMS/M	Her Majesty's Submarine
I	
INLO	Indian Naval Liaison Officer
J	
JRM	Junior Ranks Mess
K	
Kg	Kilogram
L	
LA	Legal Adviser
LMS	London Midland Scotland
LME	London Metal Exchange

M
MPA	Mount Pleasant Airfield
MPH	Miles Per Hour
MOD	Ministry of Defence
MODSY	Ministry of Defence Security
MP	Member of Parliament

N
NA	Naval Assistant
NAAFI	Navy Army Air Force Institution
NATO	North Atlantic Treaty Organisation
NSPO	Naval Ship Production Overseer

O
OinC	Officer-in-Charge
OJ	Official Journal
OM	Office Memorandum

P
PAC	Public Accounts Committee
PDC/N	Principle Director Accounts/Navy
PGC	Project Group Construction
PGE	Project Group Engineering
PJHQ	Permanent Joint Headquarters
PLEM	Pipeline End Manifold
PQ	Parliamentary Question

Q
QA	Quality Assurance
QC	Quality Control
QC	Queen's Council

R

RAF	Royal Air Force
RXR	Refit by Replacement
RCNC	Royal Corp Naval Constructors
RN	Royal Navy/Royal Naval
RNC	Royal Naval College
RNEE	Royal Naval Equipment Exhibition
RNES	Royal Naval Engineering Service
RUH	Royal United Hospital

S

SALMO	Salvage and Mooring Officer
SEO	Senior Executive Officer
SFOP	Senior Finance Officer Polaris
SCWEPPES	Ship and Weapon Departments Meeting
SGL	Stanley Growers Ltd
SPM	Single Point Mooring
STUFT	Ships Taken Up From Trade

T

TPSE	Technical Publication Section Engineering
TPSL	Technical Publication Section Electrical
TSG	Technical Services Group
TUPE	Transfer of Undertakings (Protection of Employment)
TV	Television

U

UEI	Union of Educational Institute
UK	United Kingdom
UN	United Nations

V
VTOL   Vertical Take-off and Landing

W
WP   Weapons Projects
WPIB   Weapons Project Information Book
WWII   World War Two

X
XC   Specialist Construction
XE   Specialist Engineering
XL   Specialist Electrical

Y
YJ   Yellow Jacket

Z
Z   Zuckerman, Sir Solly

DEDICATION AND APPRECIATION

I wish to dedicate this book to all the people I have had the opportunity and pleasure to know and to work with during my 43-year career in the Civil Service. Unfortunately, many have since passed away and are no longer with us.

I am very grateful to the late Mrs Simpkins for first making me aware of the existence of the Admiralty in Bath and who so kindly arranged for the job application form to be sent to me.

To those ex-colleagues still living I wish to convey a sincere personal thank you to each and every one for your co-operation and comradeship in making my working life that much more enjoyable despite working at times under extreme pressure in order to achieve required targets, deadline dates and times and schedules.

A special thank you goes to my wife Jean who no doubt appreciated all the hours I spent at my computer writing this book which meant she had full use of the TV remote control handset.

Finally but not least, I am most thankful to my parents in the way they brought up my brothers Alan and Peter and me, particularly instilling in each of us good manners, politeness, being considerate to others and always being well presented. This placed me in good stead for my career in the Civil Service and in life generally.

Mum sadly passed away on 24 October 2015 aged 93 and Dad died on 2 September 2018, having celebrated his 100th birthday on 7 April 2018, both had celebrated 73 years of happy marriage together on 12 September 2015.

Mum and Dad

Like most parents, Mum and Dad did everything they possibly could for their three sons Peter, Alan and me, maintaining a fairly strict routine without being too dictatorial. Dad felt that mothers should spend their time at home looking after their children and all the associated daily chores, and husbands should be the breadwinners. Dad even took part-time jobs between his shifts as a train driver on the railway. Mum kept the family clean and tidy and even ironed our socks and underwear.

Dad's first car was a Morris Oxford, which was his pride and joy. He even removed and dismantled the engine and carried out a complete de-coke with the aid of the Haynes Manual. Dad also built and glazed his 8'x12' wooden-framed greenhouse. His other main passion was gardening, both flowers and fruit and vegetables. He sold his plants and produce to the local neighbourhood at reasonable prices, proceeds of which went into the holiday fund.

INTRODUCTION

My name is Royston J Tucker, a retired civil servant with 43 years' service. I am a Bathonian born on 16 October 1943 in the Parish of Weston, a village on the outskirts of the Roman City of Bath. With the exception of official duty visits to the Falkland Islands, Ascension Island, Belize, Spain, Germany and various military establishments within the UK, I have spent all my working life in Bath.

This book has been compiled mainly from memory and with a certain amount of research, and includes brief references to my schooldays and a very short-term employment as a trainee architect prior to joining the Civil Service. I did not keep a diary; if I had it would have meant that writing this book would have been that much easier.

For reasons of confidentiality and to avoid any possible embarrassment, I have, with the exception of visiting senior military officers, dignitaries and certain other persons, refrained from using individual's true names. All other names are fictitious only the initials are correct.

I hope readers find my book both interesting and enjoyable reading as I have had writing it.

CHAPTER ONE

SCHOOL DAYS

My schooling started at Weston All Saints Church of England Infants School in 1947 in the High Street at the age of four. This was a mixed school and I have few memories about schooling only to recall it was a very old building with very little heating and pupils were told to keep their coats on during the winter months. Boys and girls kept in their own groups and under our teacher Miss Lassport we moulded figures from plasticine made locally at the Harbutt factory at Bathampton, just outside of Bath. We were also taught reading, writing and simple forms of arithmetic.

School meals were delivered but as my parents were then living with my grandparents only a few yards away at 25 Church Street (commonly known as 'the Batch') I went home for lunch. Despite having friends of my own age group living in the neighbourhood it was here that I found many new friends in my class who came from outside the village.

Weston C of E All Saints Infants School

When we were living with my grandparents, it was a Saturday tea time ritual during the football season for me to sit down with my grandad, sat in his upright high-backed wooden rocking chair, poised ready with coupon and pen in hand to take the football results from his wireless. I can't be certain but I think the sports reporter was Eamonn Andrews. Although the tea table was set no one was allowed to speak or eat until the last result was announced. As usual, my grandad would say after checking his Littlewoods coupon, 'better luck next week' or words to that effect.

From infants I moved to Weston All Saints Church of England Junior School which was only a few yards further down the high street. The headmaster was Mr Pickup and our form teacher was Mr Danby. Incidentally, both teachers taught my father and some of the parents of my friends also attended both schools and many were taught by the same teachers. Just prior to changing schools my parents had moved into a newly built 3-bedroomed semi-detached council house at 91 Brookfield Park with my newly born brother Alan. My parents had three sons, Peter the youngest was born at No. 91 in December 1953.

My class at infants school also moved en bloc to the junior school. So it was a continuation of friendships. On my way home from junior school I always called in to see my grandparents where I was given a homemade rock cake and my grandmother repaired and polished my scuffed shoes resulting from playing football at playtimes.

Weston C of E All Saints Junior School

The infants school is now used as a children's nursery and Scouts hall and the junior school is now the Church Centre serving the community with its many activities.

According to the 1951 census the population of the Parish of Weston stood at just 175 (89 males and 86 females, including children) compared to the latest (2011) census figure of 5,324. It is difficult to say whether this was a true comparison as over time the boundaries of Weston changed. However, this gives an indication of how the population had grown over a 50 year period with newly built council and private dwellings. Although the village has changed considerably with Weston now almost adjoining the City of Bath, I am pleased to say despite the new builds the main high street still retains a lot of its old character to a large extent. As a child I can remember Weston consisting of just the high street and the schools, shops and pubs, Cockleshell Alley, Church Road, Church Street, Trafalgar Road, Prospect Place and Wellington Buildings surrounded by farm land.

My main recollections before I became a teenager were daily deliveries of bread by Mr Haskins riding his specially equipped bicycle, deliveries of gold- and silver-topped milk by Mr Grantham in his battery operated vehicle, especially during winter time when milk froze on the doorsteps lifting the milk tops as the milk expanded and gave the birds an ideal source for feeding and ration books. I can still remember our Co-op dividend number 23239. There were also the winter deliveries of coal and coke as well as the weekly round by Mr Jones the rag and bone man on his horse-drawn cart with feeding bag. Nothing was ever wasted even the horse dropping were soon collected by keen gardeners with their buckets and spades. Other memories were the sight of chimney sweeps going around doing their business, housewives kneeling down scrubbing and disinfecting their doorsteps and the menfolk sharpening meat knives on the top step which was slate and not least the unforgettable smell of roast dinners being cooked on Sundays and the special occasion when colourful bunting was displayed in the high street in the 50s to welcome back two local soldiers from the Korean War.

One of the main features of the village was the open brook that ran for several hundred yards from the top of the high street partly covered by pavements and crossovers. As youngsters we used to paddle and crawl from one end of the brook to the other as a dare. A highlight of the year was the occasion when the junior school, with our parents' consent, volunteered the class to be casualties for the local Civil Defence Corp annual exercise run by Major Kay. We thought it was fun having to be bandaged up for suspected broken arms and legs and applied with tomato sauce and strawberry jam to act as cuts and abrasions. We did not need a lot of cleaning up as we all took a liking to tomato sauce and jam. At the end of the exercise we were given lemonade and crisps for our efforts.

Our lessons were seldom enjoyed and we looked forward to break times where the boys played football and the girls played hopscotch and skipping in the playground. The mother of one of my classmates was a ticket collector on the bus service that ran from Bath City centre to Weston High Street; she made a point of going to the newsagents opposite the school to buy her son a bar of chocolate and handed it to him before returning to her bus. Despite other boys asking for a share of the chocolate bar the boy would sit on the wall teasing us by licking his lips profusely as he unwrapped and consumed each square.

Our sports lessons were held as the last lesson of the day mainly because there were no changing facilities on the local recreational ('the Rec') ground or at the school. We changed into our kits in the school toilets and walked up to the rec over cobbled stone pavement carrying the rest of our clothes in our school bags. Over time the cobbled stone wore away our football boots' leather studs down to the nails which had to be replaced regularly before any players were injured. When the lesson was over we collected our clothes and went home for a hot bath.

Weston All Saints Junior School Football XI (Circa 1952)
Back row: P Baxter. P Eyres. T Francis. M Haddrill. P Wilson. P Anstey.
Front row: M Darling. ? O'Connor. S Francis (Captain). T Quintin.
R Tucker.

Most of the boys enjoyed football and looked forward to playing on the local recreational ground during sports lessons. The school had a very good team and I was chosen as inside right along with my friends to form the team. We represented the school in the Bath Junior Schools Football League and most seasons came either top or runners-up of the league. Our main oppositions were teams from St Luke's, St Mark's and Fosseway schools.

One of the team who made a name for himself was Steven Francis, the smallest and lightest pupil in the class and captain of the football team, in front row, centre. At an early age he became interested in horse riding and was eventually taken on as an apprentice jockey by Mr Arthur Budgett at his stables based at the Whatcombe Estate, Oxfordshire. Steven rode a number of winners but his main claim to fame was that he rode Chalk Stream and was narrowly beaten in the Lincolnshire Handicap, the first classic of the 1959 flat racing season. It was a sad day for Weston Village as hundreds of people had a flutter on the horse. The only smiling face in the village was that of the local bookmaker. Chalk Stream was subsequently bought by Robert Sangster.

Steven was made very welcome by the crowd when he came to ride at Bath races. He rode a number of winners on the course and his popularity with his supporters asking for autographs, knowing a local lad had made good, made it difficult for him to reach the weighing room after dismounting. Unfortunately like many jockeys Steven had to give up racing because of weight problems and became landlord of several public houses in nearby vicinities and maintained contact with his friends in the horseracing fraternity.

Another boy who became much of a celebrity was Roger Bannister who on 6 May 1954 ran the first ever sub-four minute mile in 39 minutes and 59.4 seconds. Roger started his running career at Oxford University in 1946 at the age of 17 prior to this he attended the City of Bath Boys' School, presumably where he did lots of his early training eventually leading up to the big event.

My brother Alan was a keen equestrian and had a number of ponies and horses from an early age. Besides winning a number of rosettes at various gymkhanas he progressed to thoroughbred ex-racehorses and rode in several point-to-point events – unplaced unfortunately. With the help of Dad, Alan funded most of the expenses (stabling, farrier, horsebox hire, feed, veterinary fees) himself. Alan was totally dedicated to his love of horses and got up very early to muck out the stable and exercise and settled them down at night. I recall the ex-racehorses Alan had were named Rubber and Red Citadel, one was trained in the north by Bill Elsey. Alan was hoping to join Bob Turnell's Bonita Racing Stables at Marlborough, Wiltshire but Alan met his future wife and decided to go down the marriage route rather than his other love.

The annual village carnival was the event of the year. A dozen or more floats representing various topics of the day, toured the streets. Local farmers and companies allowed free use of their tractors, lorries and other vehicles to tow the floats. The procession finished on the recreation ground where the best three floats were judged by the carnival committee and awarded certificates and prize money. The recreation ground also fielded a large fair consisting of roundabouts, dodgem cars, ghost train, sideshows etc. There was also a gymkhana and running competitions for all age groups which were very well supported and prizes were awarded. The beer tent was a central point of attraction.

Thinking back it was a well organised day where everyone, participants and onlookers, enjoyed themselves immensely and was talked about for weeks to come. I believe several attempts have been made to resurrect the carnival but each failed through lack of support.

My parents encouraged me to attend Sunday school not realising that the teacher read stories from paperbacks hidden between the covers of the Bible. Parents were surprised how popular these classes were. They never did discover the attraction. Three of my friends were members of the village church choir that met for choir practice on Monday evenings. The size of the choir had diminished over recent years. Attempts to recruit newcomers through advertisements placed in the church magazine and shop windows by the vicar the Reverend Rowe and the choir master Mr Bullock failed so other methods were considered.

With the situation getting desperate it was finally agreed to offer a half a crown to each choir boy who introduced anyone that was accepted into the choir. My three friends encouraged me to go along each offering me a variety of games and other items in return knowing that the boy who actually introduced me would receive the half a crown on me joining the choir. I chose the best offer which was a table tennis set from my friend Clive Dean and I went along to the next Monday's practice and was asked to sing the music scale, 'do, re, mi…' As a result Mr Bullock noted that my voice had not yet fully broken and suggested I come back in a year's time. Unfortunately, Clive did not receive his half a crown but I kept the table tennis set. The exercise did prove to be successful with six new members joining the choir although it did cost the vicar one pound ten shillings. I must confess I never did go back to join the choir.

I failed the 11+ and was allocated a place at West Twerton Secondary Modern Boys School, later to be replaced by a newly built and renamed school called Westhill Secondary Modern and again later renamed Culverhay, always retaining 'boys only' status. It is now known as The Bath Community Academy and of mixed gender but is due to close shortly.

My only love at that age was sport, in particular football, and I had dreams of becoming a professional player. A number of people thought I was talented to do this and without blowing my own trumpet I thought so too. I was fortunate to be gifted with excellent ball control and foresight. This ambition became a big disappointment to me on 18 October 1961 as explained later in this book. After receiving the disappointing news about my 11+ exam results my parents bought me a brand new pair of Stanley Matthews continental football boots. I was the envy of all my friends.

Before I left for my first day at senior school my mother asked me to go to the village store for 5 shilling coins in exchange for a 10 shilling note she needed for the electric meter. Riding my bicycle down the hill (Trafalgar Road) into the village with my right hand in my trouser pocket and gathering speed I found I could not release my hand to apply the rear brakes. I had no alternative but to use the front brakes which unfortunately I applied with too much pressure and swerved into the raised pavement and iron railings injuring myself in the groin area.

Fortunately there was no one around at the time to come to my aid, if there had been it would have caused me immense embarrassment realising the place of my injury. After gathering myself together and straightening the handlebars of my bicycle I continued on my errand, pushing my bicycle I hasten to add, and returned home with the change for the meter. I then went straight to the bathroom to inspect my injury which had bled quite a lot and bathed the abrasions the best I could. I was in a fair amount of discomfort and probably should have gone to hospital or at least told my mother. I changed into clean underwear and hid the soiled items for me to wash secretly later. I then went to meet my best friends Greg Norris and Richard Henman outside Webb's confectionary and newsagent's shop which we agreed would be our regular meeting point. We each bought a Wagon Wheel a popular item in those days and went on our way to our new school smartly dressed in our school uniforms.

I arrived at my new school on 15 September 1955 with several friends on our bicycles not mentioning my injury not even to my best friends. I was suffering somewhat from my injury as the route to school involved a long gradual up slope and two fairly steep hills meaning a lot of pedalling but I looked forward to freewheeling most of the way home. All new pupils, over 200 of us, were escorted in to the assembly hall and sat an entrance exam to be assessed for grading. I did not do very well at the exam mainly because of my injury (I was too embarrassed to tell anyone) and I was eventually allocated to Class 1D. I am pleased to say that my injury soon got better with no lasting effects and I was pleased to take part in the first sports lesson without any difficulty. The class structure at the school was A to F in Years 1 to 4 with about 30-35 pupils in each class. I am pleased to say that I was then promoted to Class 2C in my second year, Class 3B in my third year, Class 4A in my fourth year and Class 5A in my final year. Class 5A consisted of 15 pupils whose parents agreed for their sons to stay on at school for a further year to sit the newly introduced Union of Education Institute (UEI) examinations. I sat seven subjects passing in Geography, History, Science, Technical Drawing and Metalwork, failing in English and Mathematics.

Trafalgar Road, Weston, Bath (no yellow lines in my day)

Incidentally, three of the fifteen including myself were born on the same day, 16 October 1943. This set of examinations was the first of its kind to be undertaken at the Westhill Secondary Modern School and although pupils in my class were the first to sit the exam they took the four-year syllabus in only two years. I was at a distinct disadvantage of not being in an A stream in the first three years of my schooling therefore I was not educated to the same standard as my fellow pupils in my earlier years. Only the head boy was considered brainy enough to sit several subjects at General Certificate of Education (GCE) O level. I was made a school prefect in my fourth year. I often wondered without the injury whether I would have started in the A stream. I think I was too young to be considered a late starter.

On one particular occasion with our UEI exams getting closer, I remember revising for the exams with others including the head boy in our classroom one lunch time and we were reported to the duty teacher of the day by Christopher Andrews a prefect in a lower year. The discipline was such and because the school rules were that all classrooms had to be empty during the lunchtimes, we were all marched down to the deputy headmaster's office and caned by Mr Bingham. Another incident I recall was shortly after moving to Westhill, a brand new school in my second year, someone removed two chrome screw fittings from a mirror in the boy's toilet. This was announced by the headmaster at morning assembly and everyone was informed unless the fittings were returned he would keep the whole school, almost 1,000 pupils, in detention after school finished. Detention lasted for four days. I cannot honestly remember whether the fittings were ever returned. Nevertheless, the headmaster's action taught everyone, guilty or otherwise, a lesson in discipline. Such happenings never occurred again.

A lesson I disliked was the weekly swimming session at Beau Street Baths in the centre of Bath. Here non swimmers were taught how to swim by Mrs Shepstone, a little stocky lady. The other official was Mr Diamond who looked after those pupils that could swim and the few who could use the diving boards. Mrs Shepstone had a unique method of teaching. Non swimmers including myself were told to line up some ten feet from the shallow end and in turn we were lassoed with a rope and told to move our arms and legs as she pulled us in. She was never concerned whether or the not the lasso was under our armpits, where it should be, as on one occasion the lasso ended up around my head and I was pulled in like a torpedo sputtering and choking as I reached the side. This amused the rest of the class no end. There were no lifeguards as such or other officials present and Health and Safety (or common sense) was not heard of in those days. Our teacher took the opportunity to go shopping and us non-swimmers were left in the hands of Mrs Shepstone who wore a long heavy ankle length woollen skirt and cardigan and was hardly dressed in the event of an emergency. Unlike other pupils, I must say I was never awarded a certificate for being able to swim even the width of the bath.

At the age of 13 and after a medical examination I was allowed by law to become a paperboy to earn some extra pocket money. This I did before and after school.

Unlike many of my friends whose parents could not afford holidays but somehow did see time to frequent local pubs I enjoyed the family annual holiday. A week spent in a caravan or bed and breakfast accommodation in Weymouth followed by a week in Jersey. Dad took advantage of his free British Rail passes. The passes covered free travel for himself and three sons and half price for his wife; these included the BR ferry from Weymouth to St Helier, Jersey and return. I can remember the sea crossing was invariably choppy and I was violently sick after eating a lobster sandwich from a beachside café at St Brelade's Bay. Despite this the weather was always kind to us. At the end of each stay Dad always bought the landlady a nice bunch of flowers, her telling the family that we would be remembered and looked after if we came again.

Not all pupils were as innocent as they looked. One boy whose name was Nigel Fairweather, in my second year had a habit of falling asleep in class which annoyed the teachers immensely. A series of accounts started to appear in the local *Bath Chronicle* reporting a chain of burglaries taking place during the night at private residences in the Bath area which the police had difficulty solving. The press even gave the burglar the name 'Night Owl'. This went on for several months until he was eventually caught red-handed entering a property through a window he had forced open and yes you guessed it, it was young Fairweather. Apparently he had a horde of valuables stored in his parent's coal bunker and planned to sell on later. He knew it was a safe place as he had the task of filling the coal scuttle and lighting the fire before leaving for school each morning and when he got home. We heard that he was brought before the courts but was never seen again at school. He probably was sent to Borstal a type of youth prison or to an Approved School to mend his ways.

I devoted all my leisure time to football and there were very few occasions when I did not have a ball of some description at my feet. I represented the school at football, cricket and badminton and played in the Bath Youth Football League for my local team Weston Wanderers run by David Joplin. It was at this time I first met Chesney Ferris ex-Sunderland AFC and Scottish international, Ryan Wilkins ex-Sheffield United AFC and Doncaster Rovers AFC and Tim Blacker later to become captain of Plymouth Argyll and Manchester City AFC. They played for Bath City AFC in the Southern League in the 60s and often came along to give advice at our training sessions. On one occasion I was challenged to a two shilling bet by Chesney 'to keep it up' meaning the number of times the ball touched parts of the body before grounding. Chesney got up to 86; whether he lost control genuinely or thinking I could not reach his score I did not know. I reached a score of 105 and never did receive the shilling – that's a Scotsman for you!

Between my parent's house and that of our neighbours there was a sloped walkway with attached outbuildings constructed of 4'x12' stone-faced blocks on both sides. This was one of my practice areas and where I spent hours upon hours starting with a size 5 plastic football, I would aim to hit a particular numbered block I had marked with chalk, progressing down to a tennis ball to improve my skills. I recall times when my mum called me to say dinner was on the table. I continued until I had hit my target and I am pleased to say it was not very often that my dinner went cold. I was aware that the continued noise of ball hitting the wall travelled through to the house but neither parent complained. I guess it may have been a matter of at least they knew my whereabouts and that I was not causing problems elsewhere.

Science was a favourite subject of mine and my parents bought me a chemistry set with various-sized test tubes and other apparatus for my fourteenth birthday. I made my own tripod stand during the metalwork lesson and purchased allowable chemical from the local pharmacy. The chemistry set did not come with a Bunsen burner so I saved up from my paper round money and purchased one from a store in town but when I got home and unpacked it I found we were all electric. I hasten to add I knew the house had a gas tap within but did not realise it was not connected to the mains gas supply. To do so would have entailed a lot of excavation work linking the house to the outside mains. I had to make do with a paraffin operated burner that was far less affective. I did not tell anyone outside the family about this experience.

As we neared and began our teenage years my friends and I started to venture farther afield away from the village. A popular place to go was Weston Woods an area of trees and thick growth situated on the slopes between the village and Bath Racecourse. Here we built our covered camp with sticks and foliage from the woods and there was an open spring and a number of damson bushes and blackberry brambles nearby. We spent most of our weekends and school holidays at the camp cooking baked beans, sausages and eggs kindly donated by our mothers on an open fire. We made bows and arrows from branches from the trees and practiced our archery skills shooting at a target some 40 yards away in front of a steep bank for safety purposes. Also during school holidays and at weekends, after our morning paper rounds we would cycle with our packed lunches to Sham Castle on the south side of Bath to explore the Seven Sisters caves.

Sham Castle, built circa 1762 as a folly is on the outskirts of Bath Golf Club. We soon realised there was profit to be made on our visits as we came across numerous lost golf balls which we sold to passing golfers at a reasonable price to both seller and buyer. I can always remember our summers to be dry and sunny and seldom was the weather poor that we had to stay indoors.

CHAPTER TWO

MY FIRST JOB

My father started work on the Somerset and Dorset Railway, based at Green Park Station, Bath as an engine cleaner in 1936 and graduated to fireman in 1941 and because of the war years gained rapid promotion to driver. When Green Park Station closed my father transferred to Bath Road, Bristol where he learnt to drive the HST 125 diesel electric trains up to the time he retired in 1981. Unlike many other boys of my age, whose dreams were to become train drivers I decided not to follow in my father's footsteps. This was mainly because of the very limited social life he had and not seeing his children except when they were asleep in bed, due to his shift working patterns. Also the oily and dirty working conditions did not appeal to me so I decided on office work always hoping that I would one day get a call from a football league club.

Shortly after leaving secondary modern school at the end of the summer term in 1960 at the age of sixteen and three-quarters I began work at an architect and surveyor's office at No. 9 Chapel Row adjacent to Queen Square in Bath. I applied for the position of a trainee architect through an advertisement in the local newspaper. The premises consisted of first floor offices. There was a very shiny brass name plaque depicting 'Mr DEJ Kidde, FRICS Chartered Architect and Surveyor' on the outside wall to the right of the door entrance. The door was unlocked and opened each working day at 8 am by the firm occupying the offices on the ground floor – entering and walking just along the passageway and up a flight of stairs onto the first floor landing there were two offices incorporating plenty of cupboard space which formed the business premises of DEJ Kidde, Chartered Architect and Surveyor.

In my Sunday best suit (I had no other and could not really wear jeans or my school uniform) which I had 'made-to-measure' at John Colliers before leaving school only a few months earlier and paid for by my parents, and with my credentials including my UEI Certificate for Technical Drawing and several of my third-angle projection drawings which my school allowed me to keep I made my way to No. 9 Chapel Row. I was interviewed by the owner himself, Mr Kidde for the advertised vacancy as a trainee architect. The interview took place in Mr Kidde's office and whose large desk took up almost the whole area and the smoke density was such that I had a bout of coughing. At the end of the interview which lasted no more than fifteen minutes I was given the job and started work the next day. As far as I was aware I was the only candidate.

On arrival the next day again in my best and only suit, Mr Kidde outlined my duties, which were basically to follow his instructions, and I was handed a large round retractable tape reel measure and an address and told to go to a large derelict garage close to the River Avon and to return with the internal dimensions including height.

The garage with large double doors hanging off their hinges contained dilapidated rusty vehicles (cars, motorbikes, caravan, farm-trailer and an old tractor) and an array of empty oil and petrol cans.

I was not warned about the condition of the premises or asked to go home for a change of clothes. With no lighting and in semi darkness and having to cope with a leaking roof I started to measure the premises and after about two hours of climbing over dusty and dirty vehicles and slip sliding on the oily floor I returned to the office and handed Mr Kidde, a somewhat dirty measure and a piece of paper with my measurements written on it.

I stood and watched him lean back in his chair, thinking at any moment he would topple over backwards, as he opened his desk drawer and took from it an A4 size drawing. Comparing the drawing with my measurements he looked up at me and said that I was 1½' longer on the width and 1¼' shorter on length and spot-on on the height compared to the measurements on his drawing. He did not elaborate. Obviously, this was to test me and I thought I did quite well, given the obstacles I had to encounter in the garage, and especially as we are talking about a building with dimensions some 80'x40' x20' high. The height was the most difficult part but I was fortunate to find three lengths of wood which when tied together reached to the ceiling.

When I got home, my parents were fuming and I received a proper rollicking as my best and only suit was almost ruined and my shoes were covered in grease. This area of Bath was prone to flooding and the recent overflow from the river following heavy rain did not help matters. They thought that Mr Kidde should have told me to turn up in old clothes knowing that he was to send me to this derelict building. My mother was on the verge of going to see Mr Kidde and give him a piece of her mind but was persuaded otherwise by my father thinking it would not be in my favour especially as I had been with Mr Kidde for a very short time. My suit was taken to The Regency Cleaners for a twenty-four-hour dry cleaning turnaround and my shoes were dried and polished.

Mr DEJ Kidde as I soon found out was a heavy chain smoker and was in his early seventies. He had white hair with a matching coloured moustache with a scorched yellow streak below his nostrils caused by him continuously holding his Capstan full strength cigarette in his mouth until it was at the point of burning his lips. There were ash droppings everywhere. He kept his door closed at all times and the walls were stained brown with nicotine. I literally had to cut my way into his office through a thick haze of tobacco smoke. Being a non-smoker the smell of cigarette smoke made me feel sick, I tried opening the windows but the seals and frames had been painted over. Talk about health and safety working conditions in those days? A much needed cleaner came twice a week after attending to the shared toilet on the ground floor. I think she detested smoking like me as I noticed she did not spend a lot of time on the premises; she would empty the ashtray and give a quick dust over and depart hastily before Mr Kidde arrived.

The outer office contained a large easel, drawing board, tee squares, numerous other instruments, compasses, set squares and various-sized drawing paper, two four-drawer filing cabinets, specially designed six-drawer container for storage of flat drawings and four large built-in cupboards filled with rolls of dusty old drawings many of which were covered in cobwebs. Some drawings were so old and brittle that they disintegrated when handled.

It was not long before I began to realise whether I had a meaningful future with the firm. Mr Kidde was not forward with such information and when eventually I began to ask questions he appeared evasive and he would either change the subject or walk away pretending not to have heard anything. I continued to make the tea and check the mail box downstairs. The main task given to me was to clear out all the files and drawings from the cupboards and drawers and sacked up for collection by the council for burning. I assumed everything had to be destroyed; Mr Kidde did not say otherwise.

As the days went on I began to see the trees from the woods and with much effort on my part the cupboards became bare and the filing cabinets empty. During my time there I was surprised not to have seen any other employees. I never found out whether Mr Kidde was the sole occupant or whether he had made others redundant or whether they were on holiday, sick or they had left on their own accord before I arrived. The phone never rang. I did look to see if it was disconnected but when I lifted the receiver I heard a sound indicating it was working.

With no prospect of doing any proper drawing work I

decided to leave without giving my notice but not before working a week in arrears before I received my first pay packet containing three pounds and ten shillings (old money).

In hindsight, I knew I was being used as a dog's body and by sending me to the derelict garage was just a ploy to keep my interest. Considering his age I began to think whether he intended closing the business and retire and I was just there to clear out and empty the premises. This was proven when I passed the premises some weeks later and noticed that the brass plaque had been removed.

I put this down to experience of the outside world and a lesson in gullibility.

CHAPTER THREE

PAPER ROUNDS

Following my departure from Mr Kidde's employment, I returned to my daily paper rounds which I had been doing since the age of thirteen. My rounds covered Brookfield Park where I lived and Holcombe Green delivering morning and evening papers, periodicals and magazines, Monday to Saturday and morning papers on Sundays where I delivered to well-off people in Weston Road; a long road of very large and expensive houses leading from Weston Village to Victoria Park.

It was not possible to carry all the newspapers in one bag for my Sunday round so my father made a trailer for my bicycle which made things that much easier. My weekly pay was two pounds and as both rounds were the best paid by the local newsagent and as each round only took me just over an hour I had no reason to complain despite the early morning start and the heavy load, especially when it came to delivering the *Radio Times*, *Woman*, *Woman's Own* and *Woman's Realm* on Wednesdays and Thursday and the newspapers and their supplements on Sundays – not to mention the rain and snow. That said, I did look forward to my tips at Christmas time.

Leading up to Christmas when doing my Sunday rounds I rang my bicycle bell as I was approaching to alert those occupants who had not so far given me a tip. There were always certain houses who never tipped and despite my prompting I heard the letter box shut as soon as I had made the delivery. I guess they were hiding behind the curtains. Also, I must admit on Thursdays I did have a sneaky glance through copies of the *Tit-Bits* and the *Spick and Span* magazines I delivered to the old man who then lived at No. 77 Brookfield Park. On occasions when it was raining I stood inside his porch reading his magazines and when I finally pushed them through the post box I could hear heavy puffs and grunts coming from inside. I suppose this was his way of letting me know I was late with delivery – if he only knew the truth.

In addition to my paper rounds I had a small enterprise of supplying bundles of firewood to the local grocers shop at the top of the High Street, run by Mrs Gilmore. My grandfather worked at Longs Sawmills and he kept me in ample supplies of off-cuts which I collected using my bicycle and trailer and took home to chop and bundle before selling them at three old pence a bundle to Mrs Gilmore who sold them on to her customers at five old pence each.

I had a number of interview options lined up but when delivering papers to No. 68 Brookfield Park the lady of the house Mrs Simpkins who lived there with her son Richard, and knowing that I had finished school asked if I was seeking employment and happened to mention that the Admiralty, as it was then known, had vacancies for clerical assistants and were presently recruiting on a local basis. She advised that it was a secure job with good terms and conditions. Although being the largest employer in Bath, with Stothert & Pitt the crane and pump manufacturer, being a close second, I truly did not know that the Admiralty existed.

'The Admiralty', originally and formally known as the Office of the Admiralty and Marine Affairs, was the Government department responsible for the command of the Royal Navy. In 1964 the functions of the Admiralty were transferred to the new Admiralty Board, a committee of the tri-service Defence Council and part of the Navy Department of the Ministry of Defence. It is common for the various authorities now in charge of the Royal Navy still to be referred to as simply 'The Admiralty'.

I was aware of course that the country had its own navy and dockyards but did not think there was any association with Bath. Unlike today our schools had no visiting career officers to advise on employment.

Mrs Simpkins who I later found out was a Superintendent of Typists at the Admiralty at its Foxhill establishment, kindly obtained an application form that I completed and sent off. Within a week I received the date and time for my interview. Apparently, when recruiting locally the Admiralty would advertise such vacancies on the staff notice boards thus allowing employees' family members and friends the first opportunity to apply before being advertised formally in the local press.

Prior to receiving the interview details from the Admiralty I did attend an interview for a position at Thomas Cook

Travel Agency as a trainee desk officer in its Bath office. With geography being another of my favourite subjects at school I thought I had a good chance of success. However, despite correctly answering questions on cities and countries and showing that I could read and understand train and bus timetables and being told that the competition for the vacancy was stiff I was informed by letter within a few days that I had been unsuccessful and my details would be retained for future reference. I heard nothing further.

CHAPTER FOUR

THE EMPIRE HOTEL AND THE HUTMENTS

In addition to the Roman Baths and the Pump Room, the Empire Hotel was one of the main attractions for visitors to the City of Bath.

The Empire Hotel

The hotel was built in 1901 and it can be seen from the frontage that the architecture of the roof shows three buildings each appropriate to a class of person viz. a castle for the upper class, a house for the middle classes and a cottage for the lower classes. I wonder whether the John Cleese, Ronnie Barker and Ronnie Corbett sketch was derived from this building.

Just prior to the outbreak of World War II (WWII) in 1939 all major hotels in Bath, including the Empire Hotel, were requisitioned by the Admiralty and all guests were told to vacate premises within twenty-four hours. The requisitioned hotels were then occupied by personnel who had been evacuated from Admiralty Headquarters in London because of the fear that Germany would bomb the capital city. Personnel who could not be accommodated in hotels were dispersed to guest houses and others lodged with local residence in the Bath area. All told about 4,000 Admiralty personnel moved to Bath. Hutments were built at Foxhill, Ensleigh and Warminster Road on the outskirts of Bath. It was originally intended that the Foxhill hutments were built to support the Royal United and the Manor hospitals, by taking the overflow of expected casualties from the war but fortunately it was not needed for that purpose.

In the early days of WWII, although some of Bath's manufacturers were engaged on wartime production of such items as gun mountings, torpedo parts, aircraft propellers and other products for military use, German Intelligence had not identified Bath as a strategic target, unknowing the Admiralty had moved its entire warship design operation from London to Bath.

At the time, German Intelligence thought that it was just

high ranking officers had decamped to Bath and were staying in hotels. Accordingly Bath was officially designated 'a lesser town without specific aiming points' and to maintain that belief Bath was deliberately undefended having neither a balloon barrage nor anti-aircraft guns. Hostile aircraft did fly over Bath, but usually on their way to other targets such as Bristol and on their way back to Germany. However, in April 1942 Bath suffered at the hands of the Luftwaffe in retaliation for allied raids on Lubeck. Hitler targeted Bath as part of the Baedeker Blitz. These raids were focused on English cities of cultural significance and were selected specifically from the Baedeker tourist guides. In total over 19,000 buildings were destroyed or damaged and over 400 people killed in these raids over the UK. It is a miracle that despite this Bath, compared to other cities, bears almost no sign of the raids and remained to be an elegant and intact Roman city.

After the war a further 1,500 civil servants mostly draughtsmen and technical staff were to come to Bath mainly from Portsmouth, Devonport and Chatham dockyards. A number of workers who had young families who could not afford to buy a house in Bath or on its outskirts were allocated council houses. This did not go down well with those local families on the council's waiting list.

Whilst the Empire Hotel was still in the hands of the Admiralty and occupied by its staff, it was not uncommon to see visitors turn up with their suitcases seeking accommodation.

With this influx of staff and a local recruitment campaign for clerical staff the Admiralty became the largest employer in

Bath, the second being Stothert & Pitt Ltd, the crane and pump manufacturer. Bath was soon recognised as an important focal point for the navy along with MOD Main Building, Old Admiralty Building and the Old War Office Building in Whitehall, London. Bath became the centre for many functions from ship design, dockyard management and weaponry to administrative roles.

During the war the Empire Hotel housed the main sorting office for the Navy and has subsequently been mainly used by Civil Establishment branches otherwise known as personnel groups who administered clerical and executive grades and those departments who had coordinating roles to play and contained the Central Mail Office (CMO).

The hotel was the central point to all three sites in Bath. I did have occasions to visit the Empire Hotel for meetings and had the occasional lunch in its restaurant. Although what were bedrooms had been converted into offices I was surprised to see that many of the toilets which were originally bathrooms had still retained their original white enamel baths with brass fittings and ornate mirrors. I hasten to add that I never saw anyone actually taking a bath.

I am afraid that anyone visiting the Empire Hotel in the 1970s–80s would have been shocked to see the main staircase in a state of disrepair being supported by scaffolding totally out of character from anyone viewing the building from the outside.

People I knew who worked at the Empire Hotel were pleased to be able to pop out to the shops in the city centre as all shops and places for other needs were within easy walking distance.

Whilst still maintaining the Empire Hotel as a place of work, most of the staff along with the added workforce of technical and drawing office staff from the dockyards was eventually transferred to more suitable office locations at Foxhill and the purpose-built military establishments at Ensleigh and at Warminster Road. All three establishments were generally referred to as 'sites' and the buildings, which looked much the same were commonly called 'hutments'. Most of the staff was billeted locally with families, in hotels or guest houses and some were fortunate to purchase their own property and others added their names to the council waiting list.

The CMO was later moved from the Empire into a newly built office block at Pinesgate, named after the Pines Express, on the outskirts of the city centre and close to the site of the old Green Park Railway Station. Mail was moved around Bath in suitably labelled white canvas bags by black vans and delivered to central points on each site. I did not think at the time, the white mail bags were probably made by prisoners.

The Empire Hotel was vacated by the Admiralty in the mid-1990s and was converted into private residential apartments and flats with a restaurant and bars open to the public on the ground floor. Personnel who worked in the hotel were transferred to other buildings in Bath.

Each site consisted of varying numbers of red-bricked single storey buildings, commonly known as blocks, encompassed by a 9-foot-high perimeter security fence topped with barbed wire and main entrances which were manned 24/7 by unarmed security guards. Each establishment had its own staff restaurant offering a wide selection of food prepared and cooked on site. Each block comprised of a main corridor with ladies and gentlemen toilet facilities and storerooms and two inset spaces with a hot water boiler and gas rings for making tea and coffee both with cupboard-like doors which were kept closed when not in use. Off the main corridor were six spurs on each side containing offices. Spurs were either made up of individual offices or open planned space or a mix of both. Offices were equipped with desks and chairs, four-drawer filing cabinets, 6'x18' and 6'x3' cupboards, all in battleship grey or green, some of which were fitted with combination locks, and offices with wall safes. Some open plan spurs were shared by several sections and the office space was cordoned off by furniture. Drawing offices were kitted out with drawing boards and associated equipment, which over the years became redundant with the coming of technology. The head of section and the assistant director had their own individual offices at the entrance to the spur.

Aerial view of the Foxhill site (including J Block)

Foxhill hutments being on the south outskirts of Bath was the largest of the three sites and was the headquarters for the Ship Department (headed by the Director General Ships, short title DG Ships) and also housed staff of the Director General Dockyard and Maintenance department (DGD&M) in later years to be renamed Chief Executive of Dockyards (CED).

The Ship Department, also known as DG Ships, was responsible for the design and production of HM Ships and Submarines and associated on-board equipment; basically everything except weaponry.

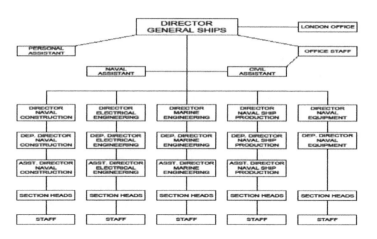

The Structure of the Ship Department circa 1960

The Department had several outstations namely, Naval Construction Research Establishment (NCRE), Admiralty Materials Laboratory (AML), Admiralty Experimental Works (AEW), Admiralty Research Establishment (ARE) and the

Admiralty Oil Laboratory (AOL) as part of its organisation.

All staff working in the Ship Department at Foxhill was housed in Blocks A to E and G and each block had its own specialised drawing offices, technical, executive and naval personnel supported by clerical grades. Each of the original seven office blocks (Block J being built much later) at Foxhill had specified main fields of work: A Block contained staff who were engaged on Aircraft Carriers and large Battleships, B Block covered Main Propulsion and major items of equipment, C Block was devoted to Conventional and Nuclear Submarines, D Block covered Cruisers, Destroyers, Frigates and small craft, E Block responsible for Naval Ship Production and G Block housed the Director General, Deputy Directors, Naval Equipment department, some small specialist sections and the Personnel Group. F Block responsible for the management of the Dockyards. Over the years further office space was required resulting in a new-build two storey office construction called Block J and several annexes were added to existing Blocks B, C and G. Staff working in drawing offices and technical sections were categorised into three main 'trades': construction (hull), mechanical and electrical and were supported by clerical and executive staff.

The department of the Director General Dockyard and Maintenance (DGD&M) with offices in Block F was the headquarters and co-ordinating department for the HM Naval Dockyards at Portsmouth, Devonport, Chatham and Rosyth.

Foxhill besides having a main gate entrance and exit gate also had side and bottom gates each supervised MOD security guards. These were known and lettered as Blocks A to G and a restaurant. The Forester Arms public house situated across the road opposite the main entrance was commonly known as Block H. Next to the restaurant was a small building where shipwrights made impressive scale models of ships and submarines which were displayed in the various blocks. Although the site buildings were originally designed and built to cater for expected overflow of casualties from World War II the site was seconded by the UK Defence Department and housed personnel mainly from Chatham, Devonport and Portsmouth dockyards. Bath being of relative distances from the dockyards became the focal point for the senior service (the Admiralty as it was then known). I actually witnessed a man walking lost in the main corridor in Block G holding a bouquet of flowers and when approached asked directions to the maternity ward. He somehow by-passed the security guards on the main gate thinking Foxhill was St Martin's Hospital which was about a mile away. He was escorted off the site by two burly security guards. The incident was reported to the head of security and a big investigation followed. Afterwards, the security guards were jokingly called matrons.

Seagulls soon became common feature at Foxhill and no one could understand why, being so far from the sea. Rumour was that the birds got confused and followed the workers up from the dockyards, as many were officers dressed in naval uniform, a common sight on the coast, and never returned.

The Ensleigh site built on the north side to accommodate naval, technical and civilian staff of the Navy Weapons

Department headed by the Director General Weapons (DGW(N)), also incorporated the Chief Inspector of Naval Ordnance (CINO) and staff of Director of Contracts and the Director General Naval Stores and Transport departments made up of civilians along with the Spare Parts Distribution Centre based at Eaglescliffe, County Durham, Naval Stores Depots at Portsmouth, Devonport, Chatham, Rosyth, Faslane and various other depots including Llangennech, Greenock and other places throughout the UK and abroad. These were the custodian and issuing authorities for naval stores and spares in times of new build, refit and emergency repair.

Ensleigh site

The site originally consisted of five blocks A to E and a staff restaurant. The site was divided by a public road where E Block was situated on a separate fenced piece of land. Both parts of Ensleigh had its own entrances manned by security guards. The site was added to by the construction of a two storey office block and a single storey computer block referenced F and G respectively.

Less than a mile from the Ensleigh site is the Georgian House, named Battlefields, built by John Wood the Younger, once the home of John 'Goldfinger' Palmer, the notorious gangster ex scrap metal dealer who swindled thousands of people with his time-share scam in Tenerife. He gained his nickname after smelting down some of the £26 million worth of bullions looted in the 1983 Brinks-Mat heist, in the grounds of his Battlefields home. At one time he appeared in the Sunday Times Rich List as being worth £300 million. During the writing of this book it became known that Palmer was found murdered at his secluded home in Brentwood, Essex. Police described the death as a typical professional 'hit'. At the time of his death he was facing charges for money laundering and possession of firearms and it was known that he was associated with the Russian underworld. His death was the latest in a line of murders and suicides linked to the Brinks-Mat robbery.

Entrance to Warminster Road site

The Warminster Road site situated on the east side of Bath housed the Principal Director Accounts/Navy (PDA/N) and staff. Staff consisted of clerical and executive grades. The site had two blocks A and B and a staff restaurant. Staff attending courses or undertaking duty visits away from Bath were allowed to go to the pay office for advancement of subsistence.

One of my best friends James Maybrick who lived with his parents at 87 Brookfield Park, incidentally he is now living two doors away from my house, started his working life at the Warminster Road site as a direct entrant executive officer. He eventually transferred to the Post Office where he worked until retirement.

PDA/N was the authority responsible for processing all pay and travel and subsistence claims for all civil servants. This also scoped staff in the Meteorological Department including those familiar faces as seen giving out weather forecasts on television. This long standing arrangement dated back to the time when it was part of the Air Ministry hence the saying, 'the weather at the top of the Air Ministry roof...'

Draughtsmen and clerical staff serving in Bath were paid weekly. Staff from the Accounts Pay Section at Warminster Road would sit at predetermined times at tables in the main corridor of each block and staff would queue to receive and sign for their pay 'cash' packets. Any discrepancies would be reported immediately for rectification. This system of payment was dispensed with when lower grade staff was encouraged to open bank accounts for the purpose of receiving pay.

Incidentally, I forgot I did have family connections with

the Admiralty as my mother worked at Warminster Road as a clerical assistant up to just before my birth. It was then known as Director Navy Accounts (DNA) and I can remember my mother saying how much she enjoyed her work.

Besides the Empire Hotel, the Ministry of Defence some years later occupied other buildings in the centre of Bath e.g. offices in Strahan House, Somerset House, Pinesgate West and Carpenter House. This was due to departmental changes and the eventual expansion of the Ministry of Defence into a tri-service organisation.

Over a period of time all Ministry of Defence personnel in Bath and other establishments in the country were transferred to the new state-of-the-art building based at the MOD Abbey Wood site in Filton, Bristol. Buildings in the centre of Bath and the Civil Service Sports Centre at Claverton Down were taken over by the expanding University of Bath and private businesses.

The sites at Foxhill, Ensleigh and Warminster Road were demolished around the mid-2000s and the land was used for new private residential housing estates.

CHAPTER FIVE

INTERVIEW AND THE EARLY YEARS

The day came for my interview, which I recall as if it was only yesterday, I arrived at the main gate to the Foxhill site as expected as my name was on the list of visitors and having been issued with a temporary escorted pass, the security guard rang through to the Personnel Section to report my arrival. I was collected and escorted to Room 119, Block G by a plainly dressed middle-aged lady and then directed to Room 120 which carried the name plate 'Mr J. Seaman, Head of Personnel'. I knocked and when I was considering whether to knock again a voice from within told me to come in. I opened the door and entered and stood waiting further instructions.

Mr Seaman did not acknowledge me at first but continued writing whatever he was doing. After two or three minutes he closed the file he was writing in and put it aside and asked me to sit down. As there was no chair close to his desk I moved one from against the office wall and sat down directly opposite him. He then began to search for my application form which he finally found at the bottom of a pile of files. Although he was seated I could tell Mr Seaman, who had a full head of silvery grey hair and could have easily been mistaken for Douglas Fairbanks Jr., was a very tall person. He did not introduce himself and hurriedly opened the interview by asking and concentrating on three main questions: Did my mother work? Answer: No. What did my father do? Answer: Train driver. And whether I liked sport? Answer: Yes, very much. Reaching the end of the interview which could not have taken more than three or four minutes, Mr Seaman rang and spoke to someone in the outer office asking whether there were any vacancies and then put down the phone and began to finger through his in-tray ignoring my presence entirely. Shortly after, the same middle-aged lady entered the room saying there was a vacancy in A Block. Mr Seaman asked me when could I start, I replied 'anytime really' and it was mutually agreed my start date was to be the following Monday. With his head down he again began to shuffle through his papers and with no mention of congratulations, welcome or confirmation that I had been given the job. I was beckoned by and followed the lady into the outer office where I completed various forms, signing the Official Secrets Act, and was handed my terms of employment and instructed to report to Mr Evans, A Block Registry at 8.45 am the following Monday, 15 August 1960, the day 'Only the Lonely' by Roy Orbison was the No.1 in the UK's pop charts – was this an omen of things to come? I asked myself.

My first impression of the Civil Service was not a good one to say the least and I thought to myself going by the interview whether this was how junior staff was to be treated by their superiors. However, I did secure a job. The interview was nothing like the one I attended a week earlier at Thomas Cook Travel Agency which was carried out in an organised and formal manner. Perhaps Mr Seaman should have taken a page or two out of Thomas Cook's training manual.

On the Monday leaving in plenty of time I took the No. 4 bus from Weston Village, the stop was just a few minutes' walk from my parent's home, taking about thirty minutes to reach the bus terminus outside the main entrance to the Foxhill site.

Reporting to the main reception office and having been issued with a temporary unescorted pass by the security guard I made my way to A Block some five hundred yards away. In fact it was at the other end of the site. On my way I passed F Block, Staff Restaurant and Modeller's building on my right and Blocks E, D, C and B before reaching Block A. There were also a number of derelict concrete gun mountings which had been left since the war and now covered with weeds and ivy, an ideal camouflage if they were wanted again.

Having sought directions to A Block Registry I arrived at 8.40 am and was introduced to Mr Michael Evans, the Executive Officer, who would become my boss for the next 6 months (probationary period). As a new entrant I was issued with a black biro, a HB pencil, a 12' wooden ruler, two sheets of blotting paper and a rubber along with standard issue bar of soap and a white towel. It was explained to me that replacement biro refills would be issued only if the empty one was returned. I soon realised that staff had scratched their name on the body of their biro for protection and some had been chewed to a point through years of use. Replacement soap and clean towels were replaced on a regular basis and telephones disinfected every week. There were registries in each block on the Foxhill site.

Mr Evans had a staff of six (now including myself). I started each day at 8.45 am and finished at 5.45 pm on Mondays to Friday and worked 8.45 am to 12 pm on Saturday mornings. On arrival all staff had to sign the attendance book which was placed on a table in the main corridor. We were given five minutes' leeway meaning at 8.50 am a red line was drawn under the name of the last signature and anyone arriving after this time was formally reprimanded and those who continuously abused the system were given formal warnings by senior personnel and told that the final outcome could result in instant dismissal. In all my time I must say I never knew of anyone being dismissed under these circumstances albeit there were the same regular offenders.

On my first morning Mr Evans introduced me to the other five members of staff and I spent about an hour with each being shown what they each did during their working day. I noticed that all members of staff were elderly, one or two I thought were beyond retirement age. It did occur to me whether I would spend all my working life in the same office but it was later explained to me that I would be moved from time to time to gain experience and knowledge of the department with the aim of eventually working in a section with more responsibility. I was particularly impressed by Iris Barnett and Miss Dinham in the manner they approached and conscientiously undertook their mundane duties. Both had difficulty standing for any length of time and as neither had transport other members of staff went out of their way to give them lifts to and from work. I was fascinated by the stories they told about the war years.

I recall sitting with Mrs Drake a kind elderly lady who on a regular basis was delivered a heap of incoming and outgoing buff coloured files, known as dockets. At times she was completely surrounded by dockets and it was only hearing her deep breathing or occasional cough that we knew she was there. Each docket carried its own unique reference. If the docket had previously been received in the block it would have had its own index card, with its unique numerical reference prefixed by a two lettered abbreviation that determined the originating department; for instance 'CP' stood for Contracts Department. So it was necessary to look in the card index drawer first to determine its destination. If the file had not been previously seen a new card would need to be created with its unique reference and other details including the subject and showing which section in A Block and date the file had been referred and similarly those outgoing dockets the cards were marked with the destinations and date. Files were then put into their relevant pigeon holes; those destined for offices within the block were collected and distributed by foot messengers and those leaving the Foxhill or for other blocks on the site were put in white mail canvas sacks, labelled accordingly and delivered by van. The delivery service was swift and well organised.

All in all this method of traceability was successful and saved many hours of tireless work trying to located a specific docket. All sacks were then collected by the messenger blue van service. Those remaining on site were delivered to the relevant block and the others taken to the Empire Hotel for further sorting and onward delivery by van to other sites in Bath or by train or courier van to Whitehall, London. Other letters and packages were franked and passed to the General Post Office for delivery.

Although Mrs Drake's work seemed mundane it was certainly an important one – the phone was constantly ringing with people wanting to know the whereabouts of a particular docket, only by using an index card system could the answer be given. There were literally hundreds and hundreds of dockets flooding in and out of Foxhill's block registries each day. Sometimes the sender failed to detail the named section on the file cover and it was then Miss Drake's responsibility to find the correct home for it. To complicate matters it was not just a job to know the section by class of ship there were separate sections responsible for construction (hull), electrical engineering and mechanical engineering specialisations. This work could only be done by someone with her wide knowledge of the organisation. In the very few cases where Mrs Drake could not allocate a subject docket to the appropriate section she would refer to Mr Evans for guidance.

There was clerical staff in other block registries doing the same kind of work albeit other types of ships/submarines and each had experienced replacements in times of holiday and sickness. Other office staff had a variety of different duties such as circulation of Office Memorandum (OM), Admiralty Fleet Orders (AFOs), later to become Defence Council Instructions (DCI), distribution of correspondence, issue of railway warrants, arranging photocopying, checking typing, processing stationery orders and other general office duties.

The time came for me to take my lunch hour. We were all allowed one hour and our times had to be staggered to ensure the office was manned at all times. I had pre-arranged to go to the staff restaurant for lunch with Mrs Simpkins and her son Richard who both worked in G Block. Richard was a nice chap with wire rimmed spectacles but did not appear go out or have any particular interests and living in the same road I never saw him out playing when we were growing up. Being under the age of 18 I was given vouchers that subsidised the cost I paid for my meals.

Entering the staff restaurant I got the distinct impression that people were looking at me thinking to themselves, a new face and another lamb to the slaughter. With blushing face (I had really fair hair then) and of a nervous disposition and with a groups of typists and tracers sat nearby having their lunch and giggling (at me I imagined to myself) I made my way to the self-service counter, collected a tray and can recall selecting my main meal of roast pork, crackling, roast potatoes, cabbage and gravy and an apple pie and custard pudding and we made our way to a vacant table. I was told by Richard that it was customary to stack empty trays with others on a trolley. Offering to take our three to the trolley in my attempt to stack them on the top of others I accidentally made the pile higher than they should be and the pile toppled over and fell to the ground with an almighty clang. Heads turned, I blushed more, must have been like a Belisha beacon even more so as other diners stood, cheered, clapped and rattled their plates, even the ladies behind the service counter were cheering.

Diners at nearby tables came to my assistance. I did not know where to put myself and returned hastily to our table. For this to happen on my first day, I thought could anything worse happen to me. Apparently this was a regular occurrence and glad to say it never happened to me again. From that point on I became a popular chap and most regular diners would acknowledge and speak to me in a friendly manner and some actually turned out to be good lasting friends. The food was very good, cooked on site with a wide choice and very reasonably priced. It was not long before I began to notice, especially during lunch-times, mature couples walking around arm in arm. I could understand much younger courting couples holding hands as boy and girlfriend but then found out that there were a lot of husbands and wives working on site. All was above board – no 'hanky panky!'

In no time at all in the afternoon, I was visited in the office by Mr Brian Bolton, the site union secretary and after pointing out and explaining the aims, workings and the advantages, especially the social and dance evenings attended by attractive young ladies, of becoming a member I was invited to join the Civil Service Clerical Association – the Union for Clerical Staff. I agreed without any hesitation recalling my grandfather's saying if it was not for the unions, youngsters would still be climbing up chimneys, however, I must say I was swayed by the chance of meeting persons of the opposite sex. Ron Brown, who along with Mr Brian Bolton, Mr Donald Bragg and Miss

Denise Walters were all active union officials in the Bath area and latterly at national level. I received my membership card shortly afterwards and my subscriptions were deducted from my pay. The Union officials were excellent in providing informative local and national circulars and acted on behalf of members on many issues. I had a real need to call on the services of the union a year or so later.

I remained in A Block until Christmas working in the Registry and when required providing clerical support in a number of other sections. This block was predominantly made up of sections dealing with aircraft carriers of the time like Ark Royal, Bulwark and Eagle. When called upon to cover for staff on holiday or absent on sick leave I was seconded to provide clerical support at section level. My duties as a section clerk in A Block involved recording incoming and outgoing papers and providing general clerical support to technical and drawing office staff. Unclassified correspondence was recorded in a plain coloured document register and all classified correspondence recorded in the red classified document register.

The Ship Department introduced a filing system that was common throughout all sections so the task of finding an appropriate place became that much easier. Some sections had a duty roster for tea and coffee making so it was not always left to the junior member of staff.

An interesting appointment was when I worked in the Technical Publications Specification sections Engineering and Electrical (TPSE and TPSL) for a few months. Each section was manned by six retired naval officers, known as technical authors. It was my job to provide clerical support which included sending draft manuscript specifications to the typing pool and when returned checking for any errors against the original manuscript copy before passing them back to the technical authors for vetting prior to final printing and distribution. Although I am not a technical person I did begin to learn the basics of several types of equipment. These sections were close to the Tracing Pool where mini-skirted girls worked under the close eye of the much older leading and senior tracers. It was here that I became friendly with Julie Reach whose father was a leading draughtsman working in D Block. The family had moved up from Plymouth and lived in the nearby Foxhill council estate.

It was possible to have your hair cut during the lunchtime albeit nothing fancy just short back and sides, purchase vegetables from people who worked the allotments between A and B Blocks before and after work and during their lunch hour. There were also two Admiralty Gardening Club shops, run by volunteers, who sold a wide range of items from seeds to lawn mowers, ladies brought in home-made cakes to sell to make a penny or two, and not forgetting Mike Osborne, a qualified tailor who worked at Hepworth's the gentlemen's outfitters on Saturdays. He worked with me in Block A registry and kept a book of sample materials and patterns in the office and spent most of his lunchtime measuring people up for suits etc. at predetermined times to supplement his civil service pay. Orders would be taken and suits made and brought into the office to be collected by the customers. This pleased many customers as there was no need to make a special trip to the shop and perhaps more so it avoided being accompanied by their wives. Mike would always be seen wearing a tape measure around his neck above his white shirt and waistcoat, as a typical tailor would do, which of course attracted custom. I was measured up for a blazer by him and was extremely pleased with the result.

I soon found out it was always wise to carry a Pak-a-Mac with me as the walk from the bus stop on the main road near G Block down to A Block was so exposed especially when it was raining or snowing. There were not many places except the bike sheds under which to shelter and more importantly the need to sign the attendance book before the red line was drawn. I suppose in the circumstances this was the best that could be done to ensure prompt attendance even allowing for some leeway but did not take account of ladies in their toilets applying make-up and doing their hair and men discussing the last evening's football match on the television. All was pretty well relaxed but everyone knew there was a job to do.

At the time of joining, the Admiralty had its own sports club and facilities at Norwood on the outskirts of Bath with adjoining football, cricket and rugby pitches. The large somewhat primitive wood built hut consisted of one large room with bar and kitchen facilities and was used for dances and receptions and other functions. There were also several other smaller buildings close by that were used as changing rooms with showers and storerooms. The club was run by volunteers and considering it was off the beaten track it was quite well frequented. Although it was open to all departments of the Civil Service such as the Inland Revenue Tax it was mainly utilised by people from the Admiralty. All this changed with the formation of the Civil Service Sports Association (Bath Area) in 1970, when club was moved to land at Claverton Down within walking distance of Foxhill.

The club house was a large stone glass-fronted building fitted out with the latest mod cons with permanent stewards operating the bar and the whole enterprise was managed by a committee chaired by Les Wilkins. Besides the normal football, rugby and cricket pitches the club had badminton and tennis courts and an outdoor bowls green and it was a popular venue for retirement parties and the like. Perhaps understandable due to the eventual move of personnel out of Bath to Abbey Wood, Bristol the Civil Service Sports Association ironically sold the ground and buildings to Bath University in 1999.

I spent the next few months or so working in several of the destroyers and frigates sections in Block D, undertaking general clerical duties. It was not that exciting and the work was pretty mundane and not as taxing or enjoyable as some of my previous jobs. At least I became familiar with the classes and names of ships which did help me in later years.

I moved from D Block to work in the main registry in E Block. The Executive Officer was Paul Meadows who spent a lot of time reading the Oxford Concise Dictionary and practising the use of new words on his staff and those who visited the office. I guess this was to better his knowledge of the English language and to impress in front of interview boards in his attempt to gain promotion.

Besides Mr Meadows, there were two other males, James Campbell, a Scotsman with broad accent who did not hold back when expressing his opinion, Mr Jenkins an exceptionally tall person and four female members of staff. My duties in this office were much the same as those I undertook in A Block registry, again the staff was much older than I was and we had little in common except for James Campbell who was a keen Glasgow Rangers supporter.

Mr Jenkins was a heavy pipe smoker who was most inconsiderate to others insisting that the windows should remain closed at all times (no health and safety rules existed at the time). He appeared to run the office and Mr Meadows did not seem to mind as long as he was left to read his dictionary but James Campbell did have arguments with the pipe smoker but nothing changed. I sat next to Miss Dinby a sweet lady who did take me under her wings to explain the workings of the registry. Again the work was routine and not at all challenging. The work consisted of recording incoming and outgoing mail, answering telephone enquiries and other mundane chores except making the tea which the ladies undertook willingly, perhaps because they could have a chat to others at the tea urn and to get away from the smoky office.

I became friendly with several lads of my own age who worked in nearby offices and in the summer months when the weather was fine a group of us would often play football on a makeshift pitch on the grassed area between Blocks E and G away from the helicopter landing pad. We used coats and canes to form goal posts and there were always enough players to play five-a-side. Some of our 'friendly' games turned out to be quite competitive especially when Andrew Millard was playing. He was a regular winger for The Old Sulians XV Rugby Team and besides being fast and having little to no co-ordination he was extremely keen in tackles with a win or nothing attitude. These friendly games often drew a number of spectators from surrounding offices that would, especially when the sun was shining, bring their chairs and sit outside applauding when appropriate and shuddered when Andrew went to tackle. We took the games too seriously at times with heavy and sliding tackles to the extent that it was surprising that no one actually got seriously injured.

The helicopter landing pad close to our makeshift pitch was used for visiting dignitaries such as Secretary of State and Ministers for Defence, members of the Admiralty Board, often by the 1st Sea Lord and occasionally the Controller of the Navy, the 3rd Sea Lord. Helicopters landing at Foxhill were directed in by authorised naval officers with bats from the Directorate of Naval Equipment (DNE), who had previously experienced this duty when at sea and at other shore establishments. Ambulance, fire engines and the police were in attendance at all times during landings and take-offs. There were a few times when our kick-a-rounds were interrupted by the arrival of a helicopter. On one occasion after the visitors had disembarked from the helicopter and disappeared usually into Block G, the pilot actually joined in our game. Thinking back, I wonder whether this was actually allowed – what would have happened if the pilot had got injured and was unable to fulfil the return journey.

Also, always present at helicopter landings was the unforgettable Mr Martin Peterson a grey haired man who acted like he was the top man, head of operations and the site manager all rolled into one for maintenance and ground work undertaken by private contractors. With clipboard in hand, wearing a brown overall he was regularly seen walking around on site giving the impression of being in charge and making sure contractors fulfilled their tasks. It transpired he was only administering in general terms as full responsibility fell to council officials who were qualified to carry out inspections and signed-off work packages as Peterson was not qualified to do so

We also played cricket and in the height of summer many office staff brought deck chairs to watch having their lunch at the same time. We were kindly allowed to use the Civil Service's 2nd XI cricket team's kit; wooden pegs were used to determine the boundary. Each session lasted just one hour and would continue the next day and so on. There were never enough players to form two full eleven teams so we improvised whereby everyone would be allowed to bowl two overs each. Batsmen would retire once they had reached fifty runs. The player with the highest score linked to the number of wickets taken was the overall winner and was presented with a makeshift trophy. The secret being was for batsmen to get to 49 runs and then hit a six making a run tally of 55. I am pleased that over the years we played cricket there were no incidents of smashed office windows or damaged vehicles in the nearby carpark especially as we were playing with proper cricket balls.

There were however the occasional injury to players, mostly bruising which were soon brushed off in order for the game to continue. There were no serious injuries I am pleased to say.

I was presently playing football for Weston Wanderers, managed by David Jocklin in the Bath Youth League and I represented Bath Youth XI against Eintract Braunschweig a German youth team at Twerton Park, the home ground of Bath City AFC who played in the Southern League. We lost 2-1. Despite the score we were outplayed. Our opposition was better organised and the players were all six footers and much stronger than us.

Weston Wanderers Football Team
Back Row: K Palmer. B Cross. P Cook. T Fathers. D Yorouth. ? Slater
Front Row: P Jackson. R Tucker. J Jones (mascot). R Hawkins. T Albin.
C Gentry

ROYSTON TUCKER

Playing for Weston Wanderers in the Bath Youth League our home ground was at Penhill near Weston Village and most of our away games were at Norwood Playing Fields. It was customary for my friends and I to rush home after the game for tea and a change of clothes before heading with our girlfriends to one of the cinemas in Bath to watch the latest released films. One of us would always buy a copy of the 'Pink'Un', the local sports paper, on the way to see whether anyone of us had been mentioned in the brief write ups that appeared on the back page. I did not know how it possible in those days, without access to mobile phones for reports to get to the editor's office and printed and circulated for purchase in such a short time.

During the lunchtime kick-arounds at work I think I was spotted by someone who ran the Civil Service football teams and I was selected to play for the first team in the Wiltshire league on the Saturday. This was on the Saturday after I was hospitalised with fractures to the left leg. This could have been the start of something good. I joined the CS Badminton Club and represented the first team in competitions against local clubs. I also played cricket in the inter-departmental competitions.

Another lad in our group was Wally Wilden, a clerical officer who like many of us at our age lived with his parents. After applying for various advertised foreign posts he was eventually successful at interview for a clerical officer's two year posting period to Aden. I bumped into him on one of his vacations back home and he explained how much he was enjoying his job, especially the social and official life in the diplomatic service, foreign subsistence was great and that he had just heard his posting had been extended by a further two years. He added he was hoping to be able to put a deposit on a house from his savings at the end of his tour. The next time I saw him was some three years later under somewhat different circumstances when he told me he had been dismissed from the Civil Service and was now working on the buses. Apparently, during another home visit one of his friends in Bath took a liking to his expensive tax free camera he had purchased in the Middle East and asked Wally if he could get one for him when he went back. Wally went on to explain that he bought a tax free camera and sent it to his friend through the diplomatic bag service. The package was intercepted by the foreign office and Wally's career in the Civil Service came to an abrupt end. I will never to this day understand why he took such a risk especially when his job was at stake. He certainly lived up to his name.

In the autumn of 1961 I was moved to G Block to work in the Technical Services Group (TSG), a Project Section headed by Chief Constructor Gregory Smith and supported by a constructor Vincent Ambleton, a senior draughtsman Daniel Chivers, a leading draughtsman Adrian Pitman and three draughtsmen Messrs Norris, Timmington and Plowman (known as Trigger). I never did find out why he was given this nickname – it was years before *Only Fools and Horses* hit the TV screen.

With just six persons to support I had plenty of time on my hands. I took a special interest on the work being carried out by the three draughtsmen. This section had the very first computer to be installed on the Foxhill site. I think it was manufactured by Ferranti and Mr Smith was the king pin. I think it may have been the forerunner or the very early stages of computer aided design (CAD). Gregory Smith never left his office even to see his staff in the outer office. He remained a recluse only venturing out of his office to visit the secured computer room or the toilet. He would never make eye contact when I took him his morning and afternoon tea, although I must say he always said thank you. He was certainly dedicated to his work.

The team was responsible for carrying out stability and inclining experiments to ensure that ships did not topple over in extreme weather conditions when put to sea. Everything was considered including sea conditions, speed and manoeuvrability, the positioning and weight of weaponry and machinery and equipment above and below the water line. This was done on the drawing board with associated slide rule calculations which the computer would eventually take over, and model testing at the Admiralty Experimental Works (AEW), Haslar near Portsmouth. This establishment conducted research into the hydro-mechanics of ships, submarines and other craft. I did take an interest and although I did begin to understand the principles the subject was really far too technical for me to fully understand. I was particularly grateful for the time taken by the technical staff to show and explain to me the various aspects relating to ship safety and stability.

Everyone up to and including the leading draughtsmen took turns to make the tea and it was here that I first came across lemon tea which was made with an ordinary pot of tea poured into cups with a slice of lemon instead of milk, sugar being optional. From the office window I saw two regulars to the Forrester Arms public house pass at 11.30 each morning and return after 2 pm. These were always the same two individuals and I could never understand why they were allowed to do this as it was years before the introduction of flexi-working and this pair always left work on the stroke of 5.45 or earlier. There was no signing out book; everyone was trusted to abide by the rules.

It was while working in TSG that I was accused of being responsible for a breach of security. The guard doing his routine check during the night found an office cupboard containing classified papers unlocked. It was the responsibility of the last person to leave the office at the end of each working day to ensure everything was secure. Such breaches of security were taken very seriously and the culprit had to write a report admitting to have been responsible or otherwise for the breach. The report would then be referred to the department's security officer who would decide on what action to take. For first time breaches the person was usually given a verbal warning. I found out in later years that a director in G Block had made seven security breaches and the decision was made that he was only allowed to remain in his office providing his secretary had locked away all classified documents before heading home. In my case I knew I was not the last person to leave, in fact I remember saying goodnight to a fairly high grade officer (who should be nameless) before I left that day. He disputed this, presumably thinking that it would be easy to apportion the blame onto a clerical assistant, but due to my insistence and backing from union official Brian Bolton, he eventually admitted to having been the last to leave the office and took full responsibility for the breach. The officer seemed embarrassed and seldom spoke to me when we were in the office together.

This came at an awkward time as I had just completed my one year probationary period. I was called to the personnel section and advised by a lady that the standard of my work over the past twelve months was good and there was no reason why I should not progress to higher grades. I passed with flying colours and nothing was said about the security breach.

From TSG, I moved and shared my time providing clerical support to technical staff working in PGC and PGE for both project groups, Construction and Engineering, headed by a chief constructor and a senior mechanical engineer. Beginning to think logically I could not understand why there was not a project group 'Electrical'; when I asked why no one knew the answer. I was not there long enough to really understand what each group did as I was soon transferred to the main registry in G Block to fill a vacant position for which the work had been allowed to pile up for several days.

I soon learnt that it was customary to address your superiors either by Mr, Mrs, Miss or Sir. Only those of equal grade would you address using Christian names but only if you did not object, think it was too personal. Most junior staff called their male superiors 'Sir'. Personally, I detested calling anyone Sir who had not been knighted and would always use the term 'Mr'. This was with the exception of the time a few years later whilst working elsewhere in G Block a clerical officer named

Major (his true Christian name) Hawkins quietly took me aside to inform me that his Christian name was Major and insisted on being called by his Christian name. He always wore heavy tweed suits obviously to give the impression that he was ex-military. It could not be ascertained whether he actually served in the Army or had any military connections. Everyone including the executive officer and other senior staff addressed him as 'Mr Hawkins' rather than using his Christian name and I followed suit. I was told that the personnel department was asked to ascertain his background but had refused to disclose anything on grounds of confidentiality. Anyway we let him carry on thinking he was of higher importance than he really was. He certainly acted the part with his abrupt attitude and mannerism. We let him carry on thinking he was ex-Army and a class above that of a clerical officer. The only things missing were a uniform and baton underneath arm. On reflection, of course, it was possible he did have a military background. Who were we to make judgement!

This type of attitude was prevalent in my early days working at Foxhill. A lot of people would give the impression that they were more important than they really were and held positions higher than their actual grade.

Working in G Block was much stricter than working elsewhere on the site. Personnel were not allowed outside their offices without wearing jackets. Other blocks were much more relaxed especially in hot climate.

In my first year or so I attended several compulsory courses including Induction into the Civil Service, Understanding

Defence and various security oriented courses. Some courses were held on site and others were residential at The Bear Hotel in Wells within a stone's throw of Wells Cathedral, Marsham Court Hotel, Bournemouth, and in Ministry of Defence buildings in High Holborn and Empress State Building, Earl's Court both in London. This was the first time I encountered the "pea soup" London smog. How glad was I to return home!!

I remember attending a week's induction course in the Ministry building in High Holborn and whilst walking back to my guest house in Earl's Court a young women came up to me and asked if I had the time. Looking at my watch I informed her it was almost six o'clock. She looked at me in a very strange way and walked off mumbling to herself. I thought to myself afterwards why she had asked me for the time, having seen she was wearing a watch herself. It was not until I returned to Bath and mentioned this to my friend Gary Bristow that I had probably been approached by a woman of ill repute who had the oldest profession in the world. I was certainly naïve at the time.

On another occasion when in London on a course I went into a Wimpy Bar eating place near King's Cross Station, taking a seat at a table and ordering my meal I took out my newspaper to pass the time. It was not long when I began to notice men coming in and after first reporting to the male cashier sitting near the doorway, passing me close by to go downstairs to the gentlemen's toilet and on their return handing money to the cashier. I paid no attention to this other than to observe men were taking longer than normal to have a 'pee' but when after my meal I needed to go to the toilet and making my way to the urinals I was surprised to find out that nearly all the cubicles were engaged and a strange mix of male and female sounds coming from within. No doubt the cashier had a lucrative business going and the takings far exceeded those taken from his normal eating customers.

Security became a big thing around this time. There was a series of security scandals which rocked the Macmillan government in the early 60s. One in particular was of interest to me and this was the case involving John Vassall. Part of my job when I was working in TSG was to price unclassified drawings for sale to foreign governments, private companies and members of the public. Drawings were obtained from the curator's office in A Block, Foxhill. The method of pricing was undertaken on the basis of square footage and whether the material was paper, linen or the more expensive velograph material. The amount of detail and man effort required to produce the drawing did not come into consideration. The same price would apply whether the drawing had only one or two lines on it or being complex involving many hours of detailed work to complete. Such requests were received in official files coincidently some that had minutes signed by Vassall who was then working in a Military Secretariat Branch in London. It is quite likely that in the course of my work I may have spoken to him on the telephone but I cannot remember doing so.

Vassall, whilst working as a clerk for the Naval Attaché at the British Embassy in Moscow in the 1950s, found himself socially isolated by the snobberies and hierarchies of diplomatic life and his loneliness was exasperated by the fact that he was homosexual, which at that time was illegal in both England and the Soviet Union. He became acquainted with a Pole who worked for the Embassy and who introduced him to the homosexual underworld of Moscow. It was here that Vassall was invited to a party where he was encouraged to become extremely drunk and where he was photographed in compromising positions with several men. The party had been organised by the KGB and was a classic 'honey trap'. The Soviets used the photographs to blackmail Vassall into working for them as a spy, initially in Moscow and later following his return to the Admiralty in the mid-1950s where he worked in the Naval Intelligence Branch in London. Vassall provided the Soviets with several thousand classified documents, including information on British radar, torpedoes and anti-submarine equipment. He was subsequently discovered and was sentenced to 18 years' imprisonment for espionage.

The Vassall spy episode was followed in early 1961 by the Portland spy ring when two Civil Service clerks Harry Houghton and Ethel Gee and non-civil servants Gordon Lonsdale and the Krugers, hit the news. Both Houghton and Gee worked at the Admiralty Underwater Weapons Establishment (AUWE) and shore establishment HMS *Osprey*. It was proven that this spy ring conspired to pass huge amounts of film and photographs of classified material, including details of HM Submarine *Dreadnought*, Britain's first nuclear submarine to the Russians. A large amount of transmission equipment capable of reaching

Russia was found in the Kruger's home. All five were charged with plotting to pass official secrets to the Russians and each were sentenced to prison for varying periods of up to 25 years.

In 1963, the Government was then faced with the John Profumo, the Secretary of State for War's affair and association with Christine Keeler involving Mandy Rice-Davis and Peter Ward, the osteopath. It was alleged that Ward was the instigator of sex orgies attended by Russian spy Ivanov and Profumo was sleeping with Keeler. This gave rise that the country's national security was being compromised. Profumo originally denied any impropriety in a personal statement to the Parliament but was later forced to admit the truth and resigned from government. This affair severely damaged Harold Macmillan's self-confidence and he resigned as prime minister on health grounds in October 1963. There were rumours that certain personnel working at Foxhill were involved in the scandal but nothing transpired.

Enquiries in general concluded laxation in security and stringent regulations were introduced and special training courses were developed to emphasise the importance of security in the field of defence highlighting and describing the above cases as prime examples.

It was around this time that my friends and I bought motor scooters on higher purchase and used them for leisure and driving to work. It was the only regret of my life as will be explained shortly.

It was compulsory for staff employed in the Ministry to attend weekly day release at Bath College up to the age of eighteen. This was a complete waste of time. It was supposed to be a continuation from our education but the tutors were not really interested in teaching us except the arts master's efforts to teach us pottery and drawing which truly did not interest us either so we spent much of the day in the coffee lounge.

At times the class got a little out of hand and on one particular morning having arrived with three friends at nine o'clock and parking our scooters in the road outside we made our way to our classroom and chatted generally to one another. The parking time was one hour and normally the tutor would allow us to go out and move our vehicles several times during the day to avoid picking up a parking ticket. This particular day the tutor would not allow us to leave the classroom until the pottery lesson had ended. When we came to move our scooters three policemen appeared from around the corner asking whether the scooters were ours. I happened to say jokingly, does it really take three policemen to look after three scooters. My two friends stayed silent and heard nothing more but I was summonsed to appear at Bath Magistrates Court or pay a four shilling fine within seven days. I paid up and learnt my lesson. I should have kept quiet like my friends.

I then moved to a small admin office in G Block. The office was headed by David (Dai) Timmings, the Executive Officer a proud Welshman and a staunch Labourite. He was in charge of Mr McIntosh, known as Tosh, the clerical officer and the custodian of Confidential Books (CBs) and Books of Reference (BRs) and two clerical assistants, myself and Miss Teresa Fuller, who with encouragement from her mother later married a constructor in the elite Royal Corps of Naval Constructors.

The office was sub-divided and basically made into two separate working areas with shelving and rows of 6'x3' metal cupboards to take all the books. Tosh's desk was within this area where he meticulously amended each book as soon as changes were issued. Unclassified Admiralty books covering regulations, instructions, handbooks and training manuals were issued in the BR (Book of Reference) series. Those of a classified nature were issued in the CB (Confidential Book) series. Both BRs and CBs were made available to naval officers, technical, draughtsmen and civilian staff. He regularly mustered and amended, as necessary, the classified books which took him all over the site. Tosh was a fountain of knowledge, some of which was of a technical nature, for aspects relating to his library of books and was well known and highly regarded by staff throughout the site. Many considered him to be a professional librarian.

Tosh served in the medical corps in WWII. He was affected very badly by the terrible sights he experienced. He had his good and bad days. My awareness of his condition unfolded on my first day with Mr Timmings and Teresa at lunch leaving Tosh and me in the office. Things were quiet and all I could hear was Tosh munching away at his sandwiches and turning pages of the *Daily Telegraph* which he took each day when all of a sudden I heard him get up from his chair and start banging the cupboards making a tremendous noise with his fist shouting out repeatedly, 'I hate you Doris' (name of his wife). It lasted for about twenty seconds and stopped as suddenly as it started and he went back to his sandwiches and paper. This really startled me; I did not know whether to run out of the office calling for assistance or pop my head round the corner to see if Tosh was alright. I decided on neither and stayed rooted to my chair expecting a repeat at any time. Mr Timmings returned from lunch and when I told him, quietly enough for Tosh not to overhear, what had happened he apologised profusely for not warning me beforehand. It did happen again from time to time and I began to get used to it. I supposed it was post-traumatic stress but no one knew of it in those days. Apparently Tosh was happily married and no one really understood why he should make such remarks about his wife.

My duties included proof reading of draft Defence Standards and other Ship Department technical publications before they were finally approved and sent for printing and distribution. This was very similar to the work I did in TPSE and TPSL some months earlier. From time to time I was asked to amend Books of Reference but Tosh disliked this as he wanted full control of his books.

When I returned from lunch I would often see Mr Timmings sat having cups of tea with union officials Brian Bolton, Donald Bragg and Ron Brown, jokingly known as the 'three Bs'. Each was an active union member and held positions on the then Bath branch of the Civil Service Clerical Association. Brian Bolton went on to become Secretary of the MOD Civil Service Union and based in London. Although as far as I was aware neither were communist orientated but I did see the occasional copy of the *Daily Worker* which had obviously been smuggled onto site. I did think it strange however that the three Bs left soon as I arrived back from lunch. I think Teresa would have been none the wiser if discussion did revolve around communism, and Tosh was too busy with his books.

CHAPTER SIX

THE COLLISION

My career was interrupted on 18 October 1961 two days after my 18th birthday. Leaving work at 5:45 pm on my 175cc Lambretta scooter I took my usual route home, via Entry Hill, Bear Flat, Wellsway, the Old Bridge through Kingsmead Square and onto New King Street but as I reached the junction with Charles Street and having the right of way a car being driven by Mr Spencer Potten, a director of Stothert & Pitt Ltd, the famous crane manufacturers, failed to stop at the halt sign and collided with me. I was thrown over the handlebars of my scooter, somersaulting and landing on the pavement on the other side of the road in the entrance to the St John's White Cross shop. I sustained compound fractures to my left tibia and fibula. I was conscious throughout the ordeal. With bone protruding through the skin of my leg my only thought was would I ever play football again and for someone to tell my parents not to worry. I cannot recall who phoned for an ambulance. I was attended to by a passing policeman and comforted by a lady from the White Cross shop who allowed me a sip of tea before the ambulance arrived.

As St Martin's Hospital was on call that particular day I was taken there by ambulance which I remember drove very slow indeed and seemed ages before arriving at A & E, St Martin's Hospital. It would have been much more convenient, especially for visiting, to have taken me to the Royal United Hospital (RUH) as this was just outside Weston Village and within walking distance from my home. I was transferred from the ambulance by stretcher straight onto a bed in Ward 3 and then x-rayed by a portable machine. Mr V S Hughes-Davies, the orthopaedic surgeon, was called back from his home to attend to me. I was in shock and did not go to the operating theatre until 9 pm. I was taken to the operating theatre still in the ward bed as I later learned that my fractures were extremely bad and any movement could have caused more damage to my injuries.

After the operation to set my bones I was put in a bed on Ward 3, and heavily sedated with full length plaster. A six inch window was cut from the plaster to enable my wounds to be dressed.

Almost all the patients in the ward were motorcyclists and victims of road accidents. Above the bed next to me was a wall plaque commemorating the death of the American rock and roll pop idol Eddie Cochrane who died on 17 April 1960 from injuries sustained following a road accident on the outskirts of Chippenham, near Bath when he was being taxied to Heathrow Airport following a concert at the Hippodrome in Bristol.

Days and weeks passed and following x-rays it was necessary for me to undergo several more manipulations in attempts to align the bones to their correct position. One such attempt was carried out by two of Mr Hughes-Davies' junior doctors. Mr Hughes-Davies gave strict instructions before going on his holidays that the manipulation was to be carried out under general anaesthetic but his doctors went against instructions and despite me protesting, attempted unsuccessfully to administer the manipulation without anaesthetic with one doctor sitting astride on my knees and the other pushing my foot towards my knee. The procedure was carried out in the plaster room. This caused me pain and both doctors were told off when Mr Hughes-Davies returned from his holiday.

I was allowed home on Christmas Eve and recalled back on 3 January 1962. During this period I got around on crutches as I was unable to weight bare on my left leg. Back in hospital my full length plaster was cut from one end to the other and with the help of his houseman, Mr Hughes-Davies lifted my leg onto a pillow. Holding above and below the fractures he moved his hands backward, forwards and sideways saying, 'that is not very stable is it?' It was the strangest feeling I have ever experienced – my ankle and foot was moving away from the rest of my leg – obviously, the fractured bones had not knitted.

After several more manipulations (under full anaesthetic, I must add), it was decided to fix the bones in position with the insertion of four stainless steel screws.

It was at this time when I worried myself silly whether I would ever be able to play football again. When I asked Mr Hughes-Davies he said, 'I promise that you will be able to return to the football field but whether walking or running I am unable to say.' He knew I was a very keen footballer and that

I had recently represented Bath Youth XI against a German XI and was expected to play in the return fixture the following April in Brunswick and had been selected to play for Civil Service First XI in the Wiltshire League the week I was first admitted to hospital. It was unknown for a player of my age to play in this league. My main and only concern was would I be able to play football again.

During all the time I was in hospital my mother and father being a train driver when his shift work allowed, visited me almost every afternoon and evening. Thinking back it must have been quite an ordeal as neither had transport in those days and had to travel by bus from one side of the city to the other, besides looking after my two younger brothers. I was also visited by other family members, friends and work colleagues.

I was fortunate to have two people who witnessed the incident and these became valuable in establishing that the car driver Mr Spencer Potten was at fault.

I was represented by my union's solicitors, Messrs Marcan & Dean of Westminster. Proceedings were taken against Potten, and he was brought before Bath Court and after hearing from my witnesses and me, received a meagre fine of £10 for careless driving and had his licence endorsed.

I must add that I was grateful for the part played by the Admiralty welfare officer during my absence from work. Also, thanks to Marcan & Dean Solicitors and to Mr Chesney Ferris ex-Sunderland AFC and Scottish international footballer and my youth team manager David Jocklin for their excellent statements regarding my ability and prospects at football prior to my injuries.

Mr Hughes-Davies was right in his promise. I did make an attempt to play football but my injury prevented me ever reaching the standard I had been accustomed to and besides, I lost my confidence in a tackling confrontation. I had no alternative but to put a close on any aspirations I had of becoming a professional player or even playing at a lower standard or level. It also put paid to the kick a rounds between Blocks G and E when I did eventually return to work.

I was discharged from St Martin's Hospital in March still on crutches and attended out-patients and physiotherapy regularly. After a few appointments I was given a walking plaster and returned to work the following month. It took me five weeks to go from using crutches to walking sticks to finally discarding all aids.

It was nearly two years before my case for compensation was finally settled. The hearing was scheduled to be taken at the Bristol Courts in February 1963 however prior to court proceedings and based on the advice of Queen's Council an out of court settlement was negotiated and agreed. If it had been decided to go to court and if I would have been awarded compensation less than the defendant's solicitor had offered then I would have been liable for all court costs. It was obvious that the defendant's solicitor also went to QC for advice.

In such cases as mine a third of the blame for the collision is attributed to the unfortunate innocent party who was expected to be travelling slow enough to avoid the collision and is reflected in the amount of compensation awarded. This really upset me as for me to take evasive action at the crossroads meant I would have had to travel at 5 mph or slower and even then there would be no guarantee that I could have avoided the car colliding with me. If I had known this I don't think other road users would have been happy, especially as it was in a 30 mph area. People were referring to the collision as being an accident. I strongly objected to this term as the cause was not accidental but due to the person being local and familiar with the road layouts in Bath, deciding not to stop at the halt sign. To me the failure to stop at the halt sign was deliberate. The law was fickle in this respect.

As my status in the Civil Service at this time was un-established I was allowed three months' full pay followed by three months' half pay before my pay was stopped altogether. Unplanned, my absence from work lasted almost six months to the day and on my return I heard the odd adverse comments being made by certain staff. If only they knew what I had been through!

My scooter was a complete write-off. I had no wish to buy a new one but I did drive my friend's scooter in heavy traffic for a short distance to regain my confidence and road sense.

Some years later, I noticed that the scar wound began to discharge puss. Examinations and x-rays revealed that the quality of the stainless steel screws had deteriorated and had infected the tibia above the ankle. After consultation with the orthopaedic surgeon it was decided that I should have a bone graph. I went into the RUH and after the infected bone was removed it left an open cavity where the infected bone had been. The surgeon had to be sure that the area was free of all infection so it was decided I should attend my own general practice every day for ten days for a litre of saline to be passed over the open cavity and redressed before the bone graft operation. I was then re-admitted to the RUH and underwent the bone graft operation. The surgeon had explained that he had decided to follow the procedure that had been found to be successful in Canada. This entailed taking a piece of bone from my hip and breaking it down in small granules and inserting them in the cavity and then tightly packing the wound with gauze dressing. The dressing was removed after a few days and with an outside dressing the open wound was allowed to mend of its own accord before I returned to work. I am pleased to say the operation was successful and that I have had no further problems or a need to return to the hospital. The incident left me with my left leg an inch shorter than my right leg and restricted movement in my ankle joint.

CHAPTER SEVEN

RETURN TO WORK

I returned to work in mid-April 1962 after being absent for almost six months and was posted back to General Clerical Admin Office but things had changed. The small admin office I had worked in prior to my absence had grown where it had now twice as many staff and had moved to a larger office in the Annex to Block G.

I worked directly with Denise Walker, an attractive mini-skirted clerical officer, who was in her mid-twenties and the girlfriend of Andrew Millard. She was a keen unionist and assisted the three Bs whenever possible.

I then moved to an office in the Annex to G Block. The section carried the title of GC Admin to further widen my experience. I never did discover what the letters 'GC' stood for, perhaps General Clerical…

The Executive Officer was Mr Dennis Price who had recently returned from three years' Foreign Service in Hong Kong. He was not a popular person as he treated his staff with the same contempt, expecting everyone to drop what they were doing and obey his instructions at a whim, as in the manner which he openly admitted he had bossed his workers and house servants in the Far East. At times there were arguments that led to him being reprimanded by the Civil Assistant Mr Tim Richards after which Dennis Price began to toe the line. However, there was friction between him and some of the elder and well-established members of staff and it was not long after that he was moved to another posting with less staff to manage.

Not that I wanted to, but my parents would not allow me to buy another scooter. My father gave me driving lessons in his Morris Oxford with steering column gear change. I passed my test at the first attempt but as my father owned the car he had priority; in fact I seldom used it for work. I started to travel to work on the No. 4 bus from Weston Village. Most passengers were civil servants working at Foxhill and the straight through service with no change of buses was very convenient.

On occasions the bus picked up a male nurse named Godfrey as the No. 4 bus also stopped just outside St Martin's Hospital. The first time I saw Godfrey since leaving hospital was him standing in the bus queue as the bus drew alongside at Lower Weston. Knowing he was an extrovert and spoke with a feminine voice with antics to match I dreaded him coming up the stairs to the top deck, so hoping he would not recognise me, I buried my head in my newspaper. The inevitable happened. I heard little steps coming towards me and Godfrey took the empty seat next to me and in a Kenneth Williams high pitched tone of voice said, 'Hello and how are you?' Well, everyone on the top deck heard this and quickly lowered their newspapers to see who it was. I have never been so embarrassed in all my life. I tried to change the conversation to make it known to other passengers that I had recently been a patient at St Martin's and that he was a male nurse who worked on my ward. I must say despite his feminine ways Godfrey was a credit to his profession; however, I must say I was certainly relieved when Geoffrey disembarked the bus at St Martin's Hospital. Other male nurses on the ward acted in much the same way and I believe this mothering instinct was a way of life for most but not all male nurses I came across during my time in hospital. It may have been an occupational thing.

Eventually I was kindly given lifts to and back from work by a car syndicate run by David Coffin, Tyrone Wilson and Tim Davidson who lived in an estate behind my parent's house. I replaced a passenger who had recently retired. The three drivers each had their own cars and would take turns on a weekly basis picking me up outside my house at 8.15 am on their way to work and dropping me off at the same place on the return journey. I paid so much towards petrol costs. Quite often we had another passenger making five occupants picking up Paddy Burton if he happened to be standing in a particular place leaning against the wall en route. Paddy always wore the same white raincoat, turned up collar and wore a trilby hat most of the time and smoked cigarettes. When we drew up to pick him up it put us in the mind of the *Third Man* and we would start humming the theme tune as he got abroad. Sometimes because of my work I could not get away in time to catch my lift. On such occasions waiting at the bus stop I was often given a lift by Nigel Wood who also lived in Weston.

Nigel had two attractive daughters, Angela and Maria. I went out with Maria who was a ladies hairdresser and was invited to tea with the family. We often went to the Church youth clubs in Weston village and on the Paragon. Time passed and we went our separate ways.

It was through Tim and Paddy that I joined their skittle team called the ADMATS. All players were civil servants based at Foxhill and we played in the Bath Club league despite the Civil Service having its own leagues. Perhaps I should admit it but on the few occasions when one of us had inadvertently left home without our pass which had to be shown to gain entry onto the site, we would either especially on a cold morning all breathe heavily to steam up the car windows or pretend to accidentally drop the pass just as we were passing the guard. In a continuous stream of traffic entering the site the guard would not stop the vehicle. We did not have to show our passes on exiting the site. This I could never understand as it would have been a double check.

I recall the occasion when Patrick Widcombe, who worked in the next office and was living in a bedsit, began courting one of the tracers working in A Block. As time passed the romance flourished and his girlfriend introduced him to her parents and he was invited to tea every Friday. After tea and around seven o'clock it was a regular event for the parents to go to the Bath Theatre Royal and then going next door to The Garrick's Head for drinks and would return home at about 11.30 pm.

One winter's evening, as usual after the parents had left the house Patrick would run a hot bath as a guise just in case the parents returned home early. With both Patrick and his girlfriend in bed together after 3 hours they heard the front door opening and the inevitable happened; the parents returned home early having decided not to go for drinks as it had just started to snow. With that Patrick hastily gathered up his clothes and sped across the landing into the bathroom and without thinking jumped naked into the bath not realising that the water by this time was now freezing cold. His girlfriend quickly gathered herself together and as she came downstairs in a calm unflustered fashion, her mother asked where was Patrick and her daughter replied in a calm voice that he was having a bath. At that precise moment Patrick gave out an extremely loud shriek as his body met the freezing water. The boyfriend/parent relationship survived and the couple were eventually married in white.

I applied for a number of foreign posts working in the military/naval attachés offices in the British Embassies including Bangkok, Japan and countries in South America. I was eventually informed that my applications were unsuccessful and speaking to my personnel department was told that it was very seldom for someone outside the Civilian Management Department, London, who happened to be the using authority for such vacancies, to be offered any of these cream jobs.

I moved to DNSP General Finance in Block E in July 1964. I was one of a team of clerical and executive staff engaged on maintaining records of expenditure taken from invoice payments made to shipbuilders representing DG Ships' new construction programme. This information was used in preparation of the Navy Estimates and Long Term Costings and forecast of outturns each year. The constant noise of manually operated antiquated press button calculating machines was a feature of the office. There was very little verbal communication except when it came to co-ordinate and produce the final document.

Up until now, the defence of the country was managed by five separate departments; the Admiralty, the War Office, the Air Ministry and the Ministry of Aviation merged in 1964 to form the Ministry of Defence (MOD). The Ministry of Aviation Supply became part of the MOD in 1971. Although many papers were published and circulated the merger had no real effect on staff working at desk level, we carried on as usual.

Chris Benson was my executive officer and other members of his staff included Jerry Childs and Brice Underwood, both clerical officers. Jerry was then the captain of Sydney Gardens Bowls Club and he persuaded me to enter the Bath Civil Service Bowls Competition with him in the pairs. Not having played bowls before I had a couple lessons from Jerry using his spare set of woods and we eventually reached the quarter finals before being knocked out of the competition. I think Jerry went on to win the singles competition.

Brice was a character, a real ladies man, tall, handsome and spoke authoritatively and would portray himself in the same suave style that of a flight crew officer. He disliked immensely being told what to do thinking himself a class above others. He wore the Caterpillar Badge in his lapel that signified he was a member of the Caterpillar Club and had bailed out of a disabled aircraft. He never explained how he gained the badge and no one actually disputed whether he had or casted dispersions about it although there was always doubt in people's minds. He would leave the office at 11.30 and return about three o'clock smelling of gin and always smoking, there was no doubt where he had been. I don't know why he was never reprimanded by Chris for his timekeeping. We knew he was married and had a number of lady friends.

Another of the clerical officers was Tom Partridge, a reserved and quietly spoken gentleman who always came to work wearing a white mac, belted at the waist with large lapels. He would never start a conversation himself but leave it to others to do so. After some digging he divulged to me that he was an author of fiction books and wrote stories for the radio. Apparently he could not write during the day so he became a civil servant to add to his royalties he received from his books and story lines. He would start writing in the early evening through to five or six o'clock then have a short nap and shower before coming to the office. He was a person that needed little sleep.

It was here that I also met Mr Newcomb whose son worked in the stables of horseracing trainer Bernard Van Cutsem. Mr Newcomb, I never knew his Christian name, was a dapper of a man always dressed immaculately not unlike a toff, passed on tips to several of the block messengers who were keen punters and had accounts with a bookmaker in the centre of Bath and would phone through daily to place their shilling bets. Not all tips were winners but the messengers could not take the risk of ignoring a tip that supposedly came from the horse's mouth, and may have come in at 20-1. I had the occasional flutter but only when Mr Newcomb told me he was betting on the horse himself. I made a reasonable profit. All this was kept quiet as it would have been frowned upon if my boss had found out.

After spending just over a year in General Finance and having acquired some knowledge on how the basic information is collated each financial cycle to produce the Navy estimates I was moved to Production Finance working with Andrew Meechan, who had recently been appointed as the technical Senior Finance Officer, Polaris (SFOP). Besides having an office in Block E he also had one office in Block C. Part of Block C was sectioned off with a separate manned security barrier control system allowing only personnel with special passes to enter this highly classified and sensitive area. I found the work interesting having to maintain a record of expenditure as part of formulating the New Construction Navy Estimates and Long Term Costings and anticipated forecast of outturn for the build of the four Polaris submarines. Vickers Shipbuilders at Barrow-in-Furness and Cammell Laird at Birkenhead each being contracted to build two submarines.

Staff engaged on nuclear submarines in C Block and needed to visit Vickers Shipbuilders were given the opportunity to apply for a seat on a small aircraft that made regular flights from Colerne airfield just outside Bath to Barrow-in-Furness. I was told by passengers who had made the trip it could be quite hair raising at times when the pilot had to fight against turbulence as it was possible to be sat next to the pilot. Others said on clear days it was just like driving a car with the pilot following the main roads to Barrow.

Compared to alternative rail and road travel, applications for seats on the aircraft was nearly always oversubscribed and were inevitably allocated to the most senior staff. The service ran for several years but was eventually withdrawn as it was found not to be cost-effective.

Other sub-sections in the finance group were headed by Sidney Hayes and Alex Tonkinson who together with Framton-Pipe and Andrew Meechan were all leading lights in the Admiralty Male Voice Choir.

It was now 1966, not only the year England won the World Cup it was also the year when Ross Polson a technical officer working on the other side of the office was appointed Mayor of Bath. Being in fulltime employment with the MOD I assumed rightly or wrongly he had to seek special approval from the Ministry to allow him paid leave during his term of office. On the other hand he may have decided to forego his pay in favour of the appointment and the status of becoming the Mayor of Bath.

July 1964 saw the demise of the name 'Admiralty' and the introduction of the new replacement title of 'Ministry of Defence'. All plaques were changed however the term 'Admiralty' continued to be used by staff for some considerable time after and is still used to this day by the older population of Bath.

CHAPTER EIGHT

PRIVATE OFFICE OF THE DIRECTOR GENERAL SHIPS

Having gained a relatively good overall knowledge of the department I was purposely selected (as I was later told) to fill the vacant clerical assistant post in the private office of the Director General Ships in G Block, Foxhill. This was one of the highlights of my early career. I replaced the son of a chief constructor, who had been promoted to clerical officer after a relatively short period of time. I think the family connection played a part in his promotion as I was informed that he was not particularly outstanding in the work he did. I was told that the post required the upmost discretion knowing that I would be handling confidential and personal and private papers and that I was to be 'positively vetted' as I would be seeing and handling highly classified documents. I had to give the names of several acquaintances for the purpose of the positive vetting process. Some weeks later a representative from MOD Security (MODSY) visited my friend Gary Bristow at his place of work and interviewed him including asking whether I had homosexual tendencies and whether I frequented with the opposite sex. I assume he satisfied MODSY as I was cleared to handle classified material up to a very high level.

The Director General was then Sir Arthur Symonds who was also the Head of the Royal Corp of Naval Constructors and besides Foxhill he had offices in MOD Main Building, Whitehall and at the Royal Naval College Greenwich where he had earlier held the position of Professor of Naval Architecture. The post of Director General Ships was a functional one which meant it could be filled by a civilian or a military person.

Sir Arthur had a supporting staff in outer open plan offices consisting of Mr Ted Ransom, the Civil Assistant (Chief Executive Officer), Cdr Oppenheim RN, the Naval Assistant (Commander RN Writer Specialisation), Mrs Sheila Summers, Personal Secretary and Mrs Rita Foot, Shorthand Typist, Miss Jennifer Long, Clerical Officer and myself the Clerical Assistant. Sheila was an excellent worker but very highly strung and prone to breaking down in tears when things got too much for her and had to be pacified by other members of staff. Rita and Jennifer were the opposite; nothing stopped them doing their daily duties.

Sir Arthur was short, about five feet six inches tall with a very round paunch of stocky build. More often than not he wore a bowler hat to work. He was a workaholic arriving at the office at 9 am and would be the last person to leave the site sometimes after midnight. He was a man of few words who would rarely engage in general conversation and seldom would he be seen outside the four walls of his office. He made good use of his secretary and shorthand typist keeping both almost fully occupied throughout the day using his buzzer to call them or anyone else from the outer office. His only pastime was to watch Somerset County Cricket when they played on the recreation ground in Bath and at Taunton. He would leave the office with a bundle of unclassified papers and work through them whilst watching the cricket. He considered this as relaxing.

I can recall him telling me that when working at Chatham Dockyard in his early days as an assistant constructor he found he could not get himself out of a small compensating tank he had entered to inspect. He had to remain cramped inside the tank for some considerable time until he was eased out with the help of dockyard workers. If I was in that position I would have panicked and have had lasting nightmares but he seemed to have taken it all in his stride.

My main duty was to record all incoming papers in a daily register, insert item into the appropriate subject files cross referencing onto a fly sheet, tabbing up referenced formers and to pass files to Jennifer who passed the files on to either Ted Ransom or Commander Oppenheim, depending on the subject matter, with suggested actions. The files then went to Sir Arthur based on importance and/or would be passed back either agreeing with proposals or with instructions such as copy to the relevant director(s) for direct action, coordinated action or provide a draft reply or to copy for information. If action was required I would make an entry in the bring-up diary to progress and to ensure that action had been taken by the appropriate date. These had to be booked out in the register. I had a fairly good, almost photographic memory which helped me no end in my job.

On my first day I was shown how to operate the 'Scrambler' telephone placed on Sir Arthur's desk. Often we would receive a telephone call on the insecure line advising that the Controller of the Navy or First Sea Lord or maybe a minister would wish to speak with Sir Arthur on the 'Scrambler' telephone in ten minutes time. This allowed whoever was available to set up the telephone in advance of receiving the expected call. In telecommunications terms, a scrambler is a device that transposes or inverts signals or otherwise encodes a message at the transmitter to make the message unintelligible at a receiver not equipped with an appropriately set descrambling device.

I also distributed all outgoing letters, memorandums, minutes, etc. having to write out receipts for classified material. Some had up to thirty addressees, mainly in Whitehall. Certain levels of classified documents had to be double enveloped and embossed with ceiling wax.

Everything had to be dropped when parliamentary questions were referred to the department. These would arrive in yellow coloured files, known as yellow jackets (YJ). All yellow jackets, some delivered by hand, came to me to be handled with extreme urgency. Firstly, depending on the subject matter I would hand the YJ to the Civil or Naval Assistant who would bring it to the attention of Sir Arthur to decide who should provide him with a draft answer to the question or answer the question himself.

It was not unusual to receive a number of YJs over the course of a week. Each was passed hand to hand and replies made within an hour or so of being received as it may have been required in answer to a question raised next day in Parliament.

It was a very busy office and everything had to be cleared by the time the courier messenger arrived in the office at 5.15 pm. On some occasions he was kept waiting to the absolute deadline time of 5.30 before he had to leave for the post to catch the train to London to be collected at Paddington Station by waiting Ministry mail vans.

Before I joined the office staff my predecessor addressed OHMS and internal transit envelopes in manuscript. I began to organise myself and soon arranged for a supply of pre-fixed, self-adhesive address labels to be made available which made my task that much quicker.

We often received letters from members of the public and one I recall came from Barnes Wallace the inventor of the bouncing bomb. He wrote in enclosing sketches of a submarine designed to carry a helicopter. The sketches were very basic showing the landing platform for the helicopter which could be lowered for storage and a sliding panel operated to seal and secure the hull. I thought it seemed a good idea but the proposal was not seriously considered presumably because of other more priority work.

Following the earlier merger in 1964 of the three individual service ministries to form the Ministry of Defence, defence business was administered centrally by The Defence Council leaving day to day running to the individual Admiralty, Air Force and the Army Boards.

It was soon after joining the office that I noticed the plethora of papers originating from the Ship Characteristic, the Fleet Requirements, and Operational Requirements committees and the Way Ahead and the Future Fleet working parties along with Withdrawal East of Suez policy papers. These papers, agendas, minutes of meeting were seen by Sir Arthur and then cascaded down to director level and beyond for information and any necessary action.

It was impossible for me to read every paper that came to me, but I endeavoured to read and understand the best I could. I did this, when time permitted, by referring mainly to the summaries and conclusions parts of the documents. All this increased my breadth of knowledge about current and future vessels of the fleet and current policies of the time.

Ship Department then employed several thousand personnel comprising of naval officers, technical staff of the Royal Corps of Naval Constructors (RCNC) and the Royal Naval Engineering Service (RNES), drawing office staff of various specialisations, overseeing staff and executives, clerical grades and messengers.

As the days and weeks passed I realised how trusting I was expected to be. I saw and handled all naval officer staff reports, annual or on cessation of appointment and the annual reports of cadets, assistant constructors, constructors and chief constructors some of which held directorship positions in the department. The reports came to the office for Sir Arthur to countersign as either second or third reporting officer or as first reporting officer for very senior rank or grades, i.e. Rear

Admirals or Chief Constructors for instance. The naval officer reports were then sent dependant of rank either to the Naval Secretary (member of the Admiralty Board) or to Director General Naval Personnel Services (DGNPS). Reports for civilian staff went to the relevant Civil Establishments branch either at the Empire Hotel or London.

I was also trusted with staff-in-confidence papers for those wishing to enter the Royal Corp of Naval Constructors (RCNC), the elite group of naval architects. Sir Arthur would chair all interview boards. These private documents included interview notes made by Sir Arthur and those summaries prepared jointly by members of the interview boards determining whether the candidates were successful or not. It seemed that Sir Arthur had the sway in deciding who to accept. I was quite surprised that entry into the corps was not solely done on the candidate's education, qualifications and character but also took into account parent's background and occupations. It was possible for a highly qualified candidate not to be accepted because of his parent's occupation. There was definitely class distinction surrounding such appointments which I found quite disturbing for the sake of the candidate.

One thing I noticed throughout my time working for Sir Arthur was the neatness of his handwriting. His notes were just as good as the personal letters he wrote. For those who were fortunate to be accepted into the RCNC were first appointed to the Royal Naval College Greenwich as cadets for training and then completed a 6-month training period at sea with the Royal Navy prior to joining the Ship Department in Bath or one of its outstations. While at sea with the Royal Navy the cadets were given an equivalent rank to their naval counterparts and allowed to wear a modified version of the RN uniform. Training at Greenwich was eventually transferred to University College, London.

Besides his day to day work, Sir Arthur was kept busy giving lectures to various bodies such as the British Chamber of Shipping, the British Shipbuilding Association, the Institute of the British Shipbuilding Association and the Royal Institutes of Naval Architects and Naval Engineers. These lectures normally took place in the evening so accommodation was reserved for him either at the Athenaeum or the Union Jack Club and a return to Bath on the early train next day to be at his desk by 9:30 am.

It was not long after my arrival that Mr Ted Ransom left and was replaced by Grant 'Jock' Tadd. He had been transferred from a Civil Establishments Branch in London and was staying in a hotel from Monday to Friday returning home for weekends to spend with his wife. Before deciding on a property in Bath and because he was unfamiliar with the area I accompanied him in his Humber Sceptre car and directed him to various addresses for him to view the houses After a week's house hunting he (and his wife) finally decided on a property in Frome Road which was within walking distance of the Foxhill site. He was a keen Hi-Fi enthusiast and owned some very expensive equipment. We had something in common and that was football; he played for Sutton United on amateur terms and we would go along to watch local games. He was a perfect gentleman who would go out of his way to help you and really appreciated me taking him round house hunting.

It was brought to the attention of Jock Tadd that someone in A Block was circulating papers from the Church of Scientology. Really there was only one person who could be responsible for this and that was Bernie Phillips, a troublemaker. Jock quickly arranged for all papers to be collected up and burnt in the incinerator. Phillips was severely reprimanded. I had not heard of Scientology before and when the aims of this religious doctrine cult were explained to me by Jock I fully understood why he took such prompt action. Phillips promised he would make this issue known to the public by writing to the *Bath Chronicle*. Nothing happened.

I had the opportunity to meet several top level officers and other VIPs in the course of my time working in the private office of DG Ships. These included Admiral Sir Michael Le Fanu, the Controller of the Navy (also known as the Third Sea Lord), the First Sea Lord being the Chief of Naval Staff, the Second Sea Lord being the Chief of Naval Personnel (and the Fourth Sea Lord was Chief of Fleet Support), various First Sea Lords and Chiefs and Vice and Deputy Chiefs of Naval Staff, Permanent Under Secretaries of State for Defence, Dennis Healey Secretary of State for Defence, Mr Michael Owen Under-Secretary of State for Defence, Sir Solly Zuckerman, Chief Scientific Adviser to the MOD, Earl Mountbatten of Burma, Admiral Rickover USN and various other foreign government dignitaries.

On arrival outside the main door to G Block, having

been collected usually from Bath Spa Railway station by RN car, visitors with the car door being opened by the senior messenger dressed in his long lapel braided coat, would be met by Sir Arthur and escorted to his office. On each occasion the visitor would be asked to sign the visitors' book.

Sir Michael Le Fanu being Sir Arthur's immediate boss was a regular visitor. On such occasions he was renowned to go missing on his way to DG's office and we would get telephone calls advising that he was in another block conversing with Tom, Dick or Harry, people who did not recognise him in civvies. It was his way of getting to know people's opinions at first hand. On every visit he would sit on the edge of my desk and chat away to me and Jennifer Long. He was not the tidiest of dressers in the world and often Jennifer had to turn down his protruding shirt collar. He usually combined these visits with calls on DGW(N) at Ensleigh, the post he had held some years earlier and a department which was now in his chain of command. I did hear the story which knowing his character I did not disbelieve, that living in Petersfield, Hampshire not far from the coast Sir Michael found out that an ice-cream seller had never taken a holiday and he volunteered and took over his van for a week wearing his gold braided naval hat while seller went on his holiday, presenting him with a good profit on his return.

Sir Michael later became First Sea Lord and prior to that he was Commander in Chief Middle East when he had the erroneous duty during the troubles in Aden. With Lt Col Colin Mitchell of the Argyll and Sutherland Highlanders having been summoned to the office of the General Officer Commanding, Sir Michael read a prepared statement to him that he had acted disloyally by not using less tough methods as he was instructed to do so by Army headquarters when re-taking the Arab town of Crater. This warning increased the rift between the General Officer Commanding and Mitchell. It was later known that Sir Michael showed Mitchell a copy of the letter he had sent to London a few days earlier in answer to complaints about the Highland harsh brutality in Crater, telling the Chiefs of Staff that he had every confidence in the troops, who were showing remarkable restraint. Mitchell was impressed by this.

The boat was really pushed out for the visit of Admiral Rickover. He was the United States Navy admiral who directed the original development on naval nuclear propulsion. After meeting directing staff including Ralph Bedford, RCNC who was in charge, under Sir Arthur, for the design and build of HM Submarine *Dreadnought* the Royal Navy's first nuclear powered submarine, a working lunch had been arranged in the main conference room with sandwiches and refreshments provided by the staff restaurant. I stood by in case further assistance was required. Whilst all this was happening, the messenger service was still operating making my work pile up. Because of my workload and other circumstances I was not always able to be ready in time for my lift home so I had to phone the driver accordingly and went home by bus.

It was my job being the junior to make coffee for the office, meetings and important visitors. In the case of visitors and meetings, this meant after ordering more milk from the milkman who delivered to the site daily I boiled the milk on the gas rings in the cupboard set in the wall of the main corridor of the block. It was always the practice for all corridors in G Block to be free of all personnel including me, when such dignitaries arrived. I became expert at this by filling up two saucepans of milk and part boiling just before the visitor's arrival and when I saw Sir Arthur disappear to greet the visitor(s) I would close the cupboard doors and run into an office close by and reappear once Sir Arthur and the visitor(s) passed and return to the cupboard to finish boiling the milk and then rush back to the office with the boiled milk to prepare and serve the coffee. I had this off to a fine art.

With MOD's move towards competitive tendering in the field of design and build, which Sir Arthur detested the thought of, meaning such work could be put out to contract with major shipbuilders and more importantly to him the future of the RCNC was at stake, it became evident that because he was so heavily involved in his work he did not focus too much on the organisational aspects of his department, in particular, staff resources and allocation and the associated running costs. Consequently, the Admiralty Board approved the engagement of management consultants Urwick & Orr Partners Ltd to undertake a study into increasing the effectiveness of the work of the department and to report accordingly. The report was received and after much deliberation, argument and discussion at senior level within the MOD the recommendations were agreed. This was followed by Urwick & Orr being tasked to look into ways to improve the organisation and procedures in the Naval Ship Production directorate.

A Working Party under the chairmanship of Ernie Twissell, Head of Civilian Branch 2, was set up to implement the recommendations which included significant organisational changes. The outcome in general terms resulted in the Director of Naval Construction becoming Director of Warship Design, the Directorates of Marine Engineering and Electrical Engineering were amalgamated and became Director of Engineering, Directorates of Naval Ship Production and Naval Equipment remained basically unchanged and a new Director of Resources and Programmes (Ships) was created. This post was filled by Ernie Twissell up to his retirement and then by a Mr Lewis.

I occasionally had a pint and a pie at lunchtimes in Block H with Mitchell Bacon. The Foresters was owned and run by Mr Butt ex-Army Major who was always immaculately dressed in Harris Tweed suits, cravat and flowing handkerchief in his top jacket pocket and ably assisted by his wife, Margaret. It was run very much like ship, with the lounge bar serving naval officer and senior civilian and the pubic bar for the rest of us. Mitchell worked in the Personnel Group in G Block. He was a likeable character, nicely spoken who always dressed in Teddy Boy knee length jackets, narrow drainpipe trousers and thick suede rubber-soled shoes. He never did say whether he dressed in this manner for his interview into the Civil Service although he did let out that on occasions he did get into a number of scrapes with other gangs when living in Bristol.

I recall one particular occasion when I overheard Sheila Summers, DG's secretary, on the telephone to someone saying,

'I am sorry I know nothing about moor-hens'. Getting a little flustered and agitated Sheila asked me to take over the call. It transpired that the person on the other end of the phone was the Indian Naval Liaison Officer from the Indian Embassy in London and he wanted to speak to someone about moorings. Sheila obviously had difficulty interpreting the Officer's mixed Indian/English accent. I transferred him to Director of Marine Services (Navy) who hopefully assisted him.

Official drawing of the CVA.01

During this part of my career, I saw many changes that not only would affect the future role of the Navy and its design and procurement programmes for naval vessels and their weaponry but also the policy surrounding the whole UK defence strategy. The most prominent being the outcome on the 1966 Defence Review, as part of the Government's aim to reduce public expenditure. This review resulted in the cancellation of various projects, including the first of three new generation aircraft carrier CVA.01 still on the drawing board and the remainder of the Type 82 guided missile destroyers with only HMS *Bristol* entering service. CVA.01 was planned to replace HM Ships Victorious and the Ark Royal and the second and third of the class was to replace HMS *Hermes* and HMS *Eagle*.

This caused a lot of discontentment and in-fighting especially between the Navy and Air Force departments and the whole of the Admiralty Board tendered their resignations as a protest against the cuts and which were later withdrawn, and Admiral Sir David Luce, the First Sea Lord and Sir Christopher Mayhew MP, the Parliamentary Under-Secretary of State for Defence, resigned on 15 March 1966. It was the main topic of conversation for many weeks to come. Further announcements were made including the withdrawal of UK defence presence east of Suez. Obviously, not being directly involved, I was sympathetic towards the Navy and particularly Sir Arthur, but took the view that after all we were all civil servants employed to undertake the decisions of Parliament and there were two basic options, either to stay albeit under protest, or resign on principle.

Around the mid-1960s The Geddes Committee under the chairmanship Reay Geddes was formed with the task of achieving greater competitiveness in the British shipbuilding industry which had declined with orders being placed with foreign companies in Germany and Japan at less cost. The Committee recommendations were approved by Government and this led to the formation of the Shipbuilding Industry Board. Despite the Government's endeavours and even the workforce setting up the Upper Clyde Shipbuilders (UCS), shipbuilding in the UK continued to decline which ultimately led to the closure of a number of shipbuilding and ship-repair companies.

If I had a claim to fame it was for accidentally spilling coffee over the jacket sleeve of Denis Healey. He was Secretary of State for Defence and was later to become an unpopular person to many civil servants particularly those working in the design area with a commitment to provide a continuing defence force and those of an opposite political persuasion. This accident occurred on one of the occasions he visited the department. Dennis Healey, Sir Arthur Symonds and all directors had congregated in Sir Arthur's office. When serving tea to Denis Healy he moved his arm and I accidently spilt coffee. Like a true gentleman he did not make a fuss only to whisper to me 'don't worry son', that it was entirely his fault and proceeded to mop up the spillage with a serviette. After the meeting I was not reprimanded as it was considered the incident was purely an accident.

In February 1966 the Defence White Paper was a major review of the UK's defence policy initiated by the Labour government under Prime Minister Harold Wilson. The review was led by the Secretary of State for Defence, Denis Healey. The document was centred on the need to support NATO in Europe and made the commitment that the UK would not undertake major operations of war except in co-operation with its allies and undertook to retain the UK's presence in Singapore and Malaysia.

However, the late 1960s brought about an economic crisis

and the devaluation of the pound, and the Government published two further supplements to the review announcing the strategic withdrawal of British Forces deployed East of Suez. Many considered this breaking point in British foreign policy and the end of a major, enduring world–wide military role.

Jennifer Long retired and her clerical officer post was filled by Fred Humphries. After the welcome and introductions I showed him the ropes as there was no handover period prior to Jennifer's departure. Fred was in his early 50s having served in the Royal Navy and leaving as a Chief Petty Officer. I thought I had seen him previously as his face seemed familiar and it transpired that whilst waiting for a post in the Civil Service after passing the 'Civil Service entrant's examination for servicemen' he took up employment as a lavatory cleaner on the Foxhill site. This is where I must have seen him. Fred would always mention that he must have been the only clerical officer who started at the bottom. Fred and I got on very well and, when work permitted, I enjoyed listened to his stories of his escapades on-board ship and ashore. He was a radio operator and proud to have served under Admiral Mountbatten during his service career.

Sir Arthur and Lady Symonds' home was a large detached house overlooking the countryside called 'Crosslands' in Bannerdown Road, Batheaston, situated on the eastern slopes of Bath and it was not unusual for Lady Symonds (Barbara) to phone the office reporting she had locked herself out of the house. This meant calling the RN garage in Brougham

Hayes for a car to collect Sir Arthur's key and take it to Lady Symonds. This happened on several occasions and I could never understand why a second key was not cut and hidden in a secure place in the event of future occurrences. I guess Sir Arthur was too busy with other more important matters.

I did not know the importance and significance of Sir Arthur and his appointment as Director General Ships. He was basically, to put it in a nutshell, responsible for the design and build of both surface ships and submarines. He was born and educated in Plymouth and was transferred from the drawing office to Bath to be appointed the first Director General Ships.

Sir Arthur laid the keel of the first Polaris ballistic submarine HM Submarine *Resolution* on 26 February 1964.

Cutaway model of HM Submarine Resolution

There were occasions when staff, having served their apprenticeships at HM Dockyards, came to work at Foxhill and Ensleigh to gain drawing office experience. Most went into digs or grouped together to buy a house to share; very few actually purchased their own houses. It was around the mid-1960s I became friendly with Edgar McGillian, Kevin Blackmore, Ricky Wilson, Mick Jennings and Luke Trump. Kevin and Ricky came up from Plymouth and Luke Trump came from Portsmouth and was posted to Foxhill with Kevin. Ricky was appointed to Ensleigh where he met Edgar from Newcastle. Mick came up from Zennor, in Cornwall to join the MOD as a clerical officer. All became friends and Edgar decided to buy a house at No. 43 Greenbank Gardens, Weston, Bath and had Kevin, Ricky, Luke and Mick as his paying lodgers and probably paying his mortgage.

Although all except Kevin and Luke were keen rugby players and turned out every Saturday for the Civil Service First XV, I had no direct working relationship with them and I first met them in The Old Crown, Weston which I used regularly, with my friends Gary Bristow, Charlie Champion, Rodney Green and Chad Morris, starting from the time when I was a member of Weston All Saints Church Youth Club, when, I hasten to add, we drank ginger beer and lemonade with our packets of Smith crisps. Kevin was a Michael Caine lookalike with same style hair and horn-rimmed glasses and certainly played on this when in the company of girls. Luke was quite a character and had accrued unpaid accounts at various petrol stations in and around Bath and finally had to travel almost to Bristol for his petrol.

I remember it was coming up to Christmas and close to the annual Ship Department Dinner and Dance at the Assembly Rooms and Luke's senior draughtsman boss happened to mention that his daughter Belinda had recently broken off a relationship with her boyfriend and had no one to take her to the function. Luke, a junior draughtsman, overheard this conversation and quietly approached his boss volunteering to be his daughter's escort for the evening. The dinner dance went well and a relationship developed between Luke and Belinda. It was not long before Luke's financial complications came to the notice of Belinda's parents and that he was not the person he seemed to be. The parents tried unsuccessfully to break up the relationship only to find that this brought the couple even closer together. However, after a couple of months Luke announced in the local *Bath Chronicle* his engagement to sweetheart Belinda. This was followed a couple of days later with a notice in the same paper with wording to the effect that Mr and Mrs Smith of Bath do not recognise the recent announcement of the engagement of Mr Luke Trump to their daughter Belinda. Things became taut and Luke left to be appointed to Rosyth Dockyard with Belinda following in his footsteps. I hope they did make a happy life together.

Sir Arthur had an office in Main Building, Whitehall and shared the services of Mrs Royall as she was also the Secretary to DGW(N) when in London.

Frank and I were invited along with several hundred staff to the launch of Britain's third SSBN Polaris Submarine *Renown* at Cammell Laird Shipbuilders at Birkenhead on 25 February 1967, by Edna Healey, wife of Dennis. The other three of this class of submarine were the *Resolution*, *Revenge* and *Repulse*.

We travelled from Bath on a special train to Liverpool and taken to the Adelphi Hotel for the reception and lunch prior to the launch. The launch ceremony was impressive and this was followed by a matinee at the Shakespeare Theatre performed by a host of stars. It was a lovely day out all funded by the taxpayer.

On one occasion I was personally thanked by Sir Arthur for spotting that he had written 'Sir Ralph Bedford' on the back of a manuscript minute he had prepared to send to one of his directors. Sir Arthur must have been given advance knowledge by telephone and had jotted this down that Ralph Bedford was to be awarded a knighthood for his services to the Navy. If I had not spotted the note it would have caused embarrassment and the minute was destroyed and rewritten by Sir Arthur. When the honour was officially announced some days later everyone in the office treated it as being a complete surprise, including supposedly myself for keeping 'mum'.

Sir Arthur was regularly invited to lunches and dinners by the ambassadors and other foreign dignitaries and was asked to make speeches at various functions.

The office received a copy of the Hansard each day Parliament sat. It was my job to tab all entries which covered questions and answers written and oral involving the Ministry of Defence, in particular the Royal Navy. Although the tabbed articles were to save Sir Arthur time not having to search for such articles I really hated having to do this chore especially when business of the House was devoted to the Navy and the Secretary of State for Defence and Ministers were present in the House.

Sir Arthur undertook a two week visit to Australia accompanied by Captain McClune RN and the resident Australian Naval Liaison Officer. With input from Sir Arthur's fellow travellers I produced a travel package containing timetables, tickets and briefs for the visit. Afterwards Sir Arthur congratulated me on its presentation and contents of the package and how thankful he was for my efforts.

I produced other briefs in line with agendas for meetings attended by Sir Arthur including Fleet Requirements and the Ship Characteristics Committees as well as the internal Watch Committee meetings and the bi-annual Schweppes meeting between Sir Arthur and the Director General Weapons (Navy) and their relevant directors.

I attended a number of interviews for promotion to clerical officer and was unsuccessful despite having a chief executive officer (a grade one below that of Principal) as my first reporting officer on my annual reports. I became despondent and was seriously considering applying for a job with the gas board. However I was persuaded to stay by Grant Tadd who arranged mock interviews for me. I was successful at my next but one interview.

Sir Arthur retired on 1968. A week leading up to his retirement Sir Arthur began clearing his cupboards of his personal effects. He gave me a number of his maths books with his name and the Royal Naval College Greenwich stamped on the inside covers. I knew it was most unlikely that he would have a need to use the books in retirement and as there would definitely be no chance that I would ever have need to refer to them I treated them as mementos and was thankful he thought of me. In line with Royal Naval tradition Sir Arthur was towed off the Foxhill site in his big black Riley car by his directors and to the cheers of hundreds of staff lining the route and a series of hip-hip hoorays. It was quite a spectacle. The secretaries and many other female staff had tears in their eyes.

An honorary degree (DSc) was conferred on Sir Arthur by

the University of Bath in 1974. Besides occupying a very busy position Sir Arthur was also President of the local Percy Boy's Club and took particular interest in the activities.

Leading up to Easter I met Sir Arthur in the corridor as he was leaving a director's office and he asked whether I knew why it was so quiet as there was no sign of any people. I had to explain that all staff had left at lunchtime as the afternoon was the start of a public holiday. Sir Arthur was so engrossed in his work that he was oblivious to such circumstances. He did follow up by asking why I was still there. I replied explaining all my work had to be completed before I was allowed to leave. He smiled and returned to his office.

During the Cold War period it was rumoured that public houses (the Forrester's Arms and the Horseshoe in particular) near to MOD Foxhill site, which during lunchtimes were packed to the hilt with civil servants and naval officers, were being infiltrated by Russian spies to pick up any loose talk. All members of staff were warned and informed to be vigilant and to report anything untoward.

Sir Arthur was replaced by Vice Admiral Sir George Raper again a very pleasant person with bushy eyebrows and about Sir Arthur's height who I had never seen flustered or annoyed. He previously held the post of Director of Marine Engineering. The changeover was seamless and our supporting role continued as before, with one exception and that was Sir George was much more prominent and was seen more in our outer office compared to Sir Arthur. It was not long after that I transferred back to Block E, where I was seen to be doing a really worthwhile job dealing with the fleet.

In general I found senior and top management and most visiting dignitaries to be considerate and polite towards junior staff but this did not apply to the likes of a few middle management grades who at times treated junior staff obnoxiously and without thought. Some even treated their staff as something they had accidentally picked up when walking in the street. In these cases I don't think their staff excelled themselves workwise in return.

Although not compulsory the clerical staff were expected to stay behind after work to serve drinks at farewell parties to senior officers (assistant directors and above) and other serving foreign officers attached to the department on occasions of retirement or leaving the department. All types of spirits, mixers and sherry were served from 5.30 to 7 pm. Drinks came from the Foxhill Mess run by a naval officer from DNE. Without fail there were always the same persons first in the queue waiting to be served and normally consumed over their fair share of drink compared to the person that made do with a glass of sherry. I found this to be unfair as everyone who attended was charged the same amount. Although drinks came from the NAAFI and was tax-free, each bottle was marked before and at the end of the farewell party and the total amount consumed was costed and then divided by the number of attendees and each person was sent an invoice. It was a perk because the clerical staff was allowed to purchase quantities of spirits at discounted prices at Christmas. I recall the farewell party given to an Australian Naval Liaison Officer who in his farewell speech referred to the make of toilet paper in the gents' loo, which was Izal with a square on each sheet, and asked whether he was expected to initial each sheet in the square after use and to send it to the Empire Hotel for accounting purposes.

On the subject of toilet facilities, each block had one toilet marked 'Senior Officers' Toilet' in the close proximity to their offices. The toilet was identical to all other toilets in the block and I could never understand why there was a need for a separate facility. I could only think it was a matter of convenience (sorry, a play on words!).

CHAPTER NINE

PRODUCTION

In the summer of 1968, I was transferred to another ship production section in E Block as an additional clerical support but this had nothing to do with finance. The section was headed by Brendan Mercer who was recruited specially from Cammell Laird, Shipbuilders because of his experience and depth of knowledge of the shipbuilding industry.

Besides Mr Mercer and I the section was staffed by Stuart Pope ex-British Railways Engineering Works, Swindon, Dickie Westcombe ex-Stothert & Pitt of Bath and Roger Jones ex-Dockyard and a keen footballer. All were technical grades. So the section was well endowed with people from the commercial world. Clerical support was provided by Jessie, a wheelchair bound spinster who travelled to and from work in her covered three wheeled invalid's carriage. Despite her disposition I never once heard her complain about the work although she did occasionally get a little annoyed under her breadth when she was limited and unable to do things an abled person could do, otherwise she was a very independent person and well conversant with the workings of the section.

Everyone welcomed me with open arms and I was soon on Christian name terms with all members of the team. The section dealt with pumps manufactured by Glasgow based companies G & J Weir of Cathcart and Drysdales of Yoker (later to become Weir Pumps Ltd), Stothert & Pitt of Bath, Worthington Simpson of Newark, Alpha Laval and other less known manufacturers. This being in the days of steam powered RN ships the section was kept very busy ensuring manufacture and repair of pumps were progressed and completed and any inherent defects found would be investigated, identified and rectified as quickly as possible without compromising cost, performance, or quality.

Brendan was the type that if he thought, irrespective of grade, that a person was capable of undertaking certain work above that of his/her station he would ask the person to do it on the basis that ability and capability would find its own level in the course of time.

Shop Floor at Weir Pumps Ltd, Cathcart, Glasgow

Shortly after my arrival, the Ministry introduced the 'Refit by Replacement' policy which basically meant ships and submarines entering refit (short or long term) or docking for essential defects (DEDs) would by adhering to configuration control have an equipment waiting alongside ready to be installed when the 'old' item was removed.

I was responsible for raising Job Identity Numbers (JINs) under the umbrella of the MOD contract and to telex Weirs instructing them to undertake either the repair, subject to acceptance of quoted price, or a pre-installation test of various types of main feed and extraction pumps of their origin.

My instructions to the contractor were by means of a unique JIN and such would be in the following standard format:

a. Pump Type i.e. TWL 20 Main Feed Pump;

b. DSME Index No. ABCDE (allocated by DGST(N);

c. Ex-ship i.e. Guided Missile Destroyer (HMS *Kent*;

d. Ex-Portsmouth Dockyard;

e. ETA – 10 days from date of telex; and

f. Pump to be stripped and MOD advised in the form of a quotation listing items that were salvageable, scrapped, items, items considered beyond economical repair and the cost of the repair and emphasising on no account should repair commence without the written consent of MOD.

If a pump was deemed to be beyond economical repair the relevant departments would be informed and a decision made whether or not to contract for a new replacement pump. It was generally the rule if the cost of repair was above 70 per cent of the price for a new manufacture the pump would be deemed beyond economical repair and instructions issued to the contractor to scrap the pump to the best advantage to the Crown.

Similar instructions were issued for pumps that required a seven hour pre-installation test prior to being issued to ship or submarine. On completion of test a formal quotation would be forwarded to the Ministry for consideration and requesting, date required and consigning address (dockyard/ship), a firm price quotation for the test having been previously agreed under the terms of the contract, delivered or ex-works. The delivery for pumps requiring a pre-installation test followed the 'just in time' philosophy.

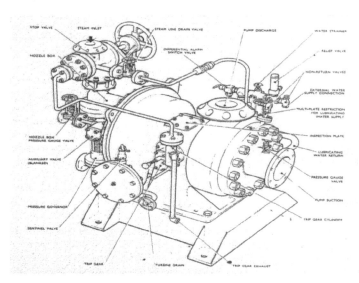

General Arrangement of TWL20 Main Feed Pump – Manufactured by Weir Pumps Ltd, Cathcart, Glasgow

My contact at Weir was Jock Scott. He had a broad Glaswegian accent and initially I tended to communicate with him by telex as I had great difficulty understanding him on the telephone.

Another point of contact at Weir was Walter Dancey, an engineer who said he was so familiar with the sounds of various pumps of Weir manufacture that he could name the actual type of submarine if one was in the vicinity by putting his ear close to the waters of the Firth of Forth and listening to its vibrations. Whether this was true or a porky-pie was never proven. I was of the opinion it was a tall story especially as noise signatories from submarines were highly secretive and such levels kept to an absolute minimum. No one ever saw Russian spies lining the coast bearing their ears to the water.

I attended regular progress meetings with Brendan Mercer at Weir's offices in Cathcart often taking with us pump parts, drawings etc. On such occasions Bernard would collect me from Weston Village in his car and drive to Heathrow for the early morning flight to Glasgow. The very first flight to Glasgow was by propeller-driven Vanguard aircraft. I declined Brendan's offer to have a window seat and took the aisle seat. Early in the flight Brendan, presumably noting my white knuckled hands tightly gripping the arms of the seat and refusing a cup of coffee and refreshments offered by the stewardess, asked whether I had flown before as I was trying, silly as it may seem, to level out the plane when it banked by adjusting my body. I replied that this was my first flight and he grinned and returned to his newspaper. I became more relaxed when the Trident series of aircraft came into service.

On arrival at Glasgow we would be picked up by RN car and taken to Weir's factory. The visit usually started with a tour of the shop floor and test bays before commencing with the progress meeting. I found standing next to a pump on test with jets of steam coming from all directions most nerve racking although workers moved about confidently and took everything in their stride. If after the progress meeting there was no other business to attend to we would return on the late afternoon flight and I would be back at home by 8 o'clock. If there was other business to attend to we would stay over at the Devonshire Hotel. The working relationship between Brendan and Brent Cousins, the works manager was kept entirely separate to their outside interests and sometimes when in Scotland Bernard was invited to a round at golf at Brent's golf club. I walked around the course and witnessed a fairly high standard of golf. The invitation was reversed when Brent came to Bath.

Despite several previously unsuccessful attempts at interview I was finally promoted to clerical officer on 19 May 1969 and was pleased to be appointed in situ.

I heard amusing stories from staff about their time in the dockyards. A couple of instances were when someone working in the drawing office at Portsmouth went to the stores department for a thermometer to take the outside temperature by dangling it from his window and when he pulled the string to retrieve it, the thermometer had gone and been replaced by a piece of wood. Most workers in the dockyards travelled to work on bicycles and parked them in the racks provided. I was told by an ex-Devonport draughtsman that because of the size of the dockyard for those who did not have bikes it was common place for them to take bikes from the racks to get from A to B and on arrival at point B to push them into the docks and take other bikes for the return journey and to leave them in the same rack from where the first bike was taken. This practice confused a number of owners and left them scratching their heads when they came to collect their bikes at the end of the day only to find that their bikes were nowhere to be seen. It was only when the docks were drained for ship refits that the missing bikes were found along with thousands of pounds worth of discarded scaffolding that the Ministry hired that should have been returned to the scaffolding company. This led to bikes being secured by lock and chain and instructions issued that all scaffolding was to be properly accounted for and returned after use.

Bertram Wilkes, the Assistant Director/Naval Ship Production set up a Vendor Rating Working Party chaired by Mr Pilkington, Naval Ship Production Overseer, South West, with Brendan and several other technical grades from the factory overseeing areas and Mr Dorkin a senior executive officer from the contracts department at Ensleigh and I appointed as its secretary to complete the working party. For me to be appointed secretary must have been unique for anyone of my grade. The Working Party was tasked to develop a process for establishing company performance under headings such as housekeeping, quality, delivery, etc. and to carry out regular assessments and monitoring processes to establish a robust Vender Rating System suitable for implementation by MOD(N).

Prior to the first meeting taking place at the Empire Hotel I came up with the idea of setting up a microphone and tape recorder which would hopefully help me in writing up the minutes. What a shambles this turned out to be. Although each member of the working party introduced themselves by name at the start of the meeting, when I played the recording back at the end I did not know who was speaking. I certainly did not recognise any of their voices except that of Brendan with his Scouse accent. It was a good job that I took notes and Brendan and I tried to make sense of the recording. After much deliberation we eventually finalised the minutes that were approved by the chairman and distributed. There was a large amount of research needed which fell to me, for the working party to reach its recommendations and to formulate the best course of action for rating companies.

The section had regular meetings with Weirs at Ensleigh. One meeting was convened with the company's top management present to discuss poor product quality. The meeting was chaired by Bertram Wilkes and it was not long before the meeting became heated resulting in Mr Wilkes producing a spindle and rolling it down the table questioning whether it had been made by a qualified machinist. Because of its tapered shape the spindle almost ended up in the lap of the works director. This was followed by the chairman tossing a small housing plate onto the table saying he would be embarrassed to offer it to a hippy as a medallion. It was obvious even to a layman that the items were definitely not to specification. The tone of the meeting improved and was concluded after the company's director apologised for the poor workmanship and promising that a thorough investigation would take place and the Ministry would be kept fully updated.

Ministry work undertaken by Weirs was sufficient to warrant two resident technical officers from the staff of the Naval Ship Production Overseer, Scotland and North of Ireland from offices at Dowanhill, Glasgow.

All overseeing staff came under the Director of Naval Ship Production (Captain Bob Hobson, RN). Overseeing staff resident with shipbuilders such as Vickers, Cammell Laird and those on the Tyne, Forth and Clyde were under the control of the Principle Naval Overseer and staff resident at commercial factories engaged on manufacture of defence equipment reported to the relevant Naval Ship Production Overseer. The overseeing service was present in certain areas throughout the UK.

The Ministry became aware that industry was experiencing serious problems producing gunmetal castings. This came to light initially when Wadsworth and Janes Castings Ltd were unable to manufacture and supply compressors to the RN ships because of technical difficulties. Accordingly, Brendan under the authority of Bertram Wilkes was tasked to undertake an investigation with the aim of coming up with a solution. Brendan visited many foundries up and down the country to establish methods used and discovered none actually knew how to produce a perfect casting. It was hit or miss and as the

Ministry was being charged for rejects a quick solution was necessary. In conjunction with the British Non-Ferrous Metals Association and after months of discussions and sample testing it was eventually realised to produce the perfect casting required an arithmetical approach and a systematic method of ranging, feeding and gating. The calculations were established and the method proven which became the norm and the commonly accepted practice throughout the industry.

One of the most rewarding parts of my work was my involvement associated with Operational Defects (OPDEFs) received from HM vessels at sea, home and abroad. Such defects that could not be rectified by ships staff utilising carried on-board spares (if held) ranged from the need to urgently supply parts, sub-assemblies or even complete replacement pumps. OPDEFs would be sent by urgent signal to the relevant ship group such as 'D' Group for destroyers (county class) and frigates (Y100, Y136 and Y160). My contact in 'D' Group was Lt Cdr Jason Babbage. The signal would be copied to my section and I would discuss the requirement with the naval officer and agree the way forward keeping Brendan informed at all times. If it was agreed a complete replacement pump was to be supplied, urgent arrangements would be made for the unit ex-RN Depot to be forwarded to Weir for a seven hour pre-installation test prior to being (for instance) airfreighted to Gibraltar and the defective pump returned for possible repair. On such occasions Weir engineers would often assist with the installation. All such work was contractually covered under the terms of the umbrella contact and by the JIN raised by me.

Several people intimated that they were surprised with the level of responsibility that my work entailed especially noting that I had undertaken these duties as a clerical assistant prior to being promoted in situ to clerical officer. I would respond saying that I always had senior staff to refer to for advice and that I certainly preferred this type of work rather than being in a registry. Perhaps, I would not have been so fortunate if a staff manpower inspection team had visited and found my post should be occupied by a person of a higher grade. It was most unlikely I would have been promoted in situ albeit I had proven myself efficient doing the work as reflected by my annual staff reports.

I remember Mr Wilkes telling me when I was standing in for his personal assistant Mrs Lipton, that he had just interviewed an overseer (technical grade) who was objecting to a move by saying that although he had been in the same post for the last ten years he still had a lot to learn. My Wilkes advised him that he had really been in the post for two years which included a year's learning curve and the remaining eight years was a duplication of his second year's work. Meaning that everyone should be fully acquainted with their job in two years and then be moved on for further experience. I eventually found out that the person was moved.

I looked forward to the section's Christmas party which was normally held in a nearby pub. A regular occurrence was to watch and hear Mr Wilkes' rendition of 'To be a Farmer's Boy'. Mr Wilkes' styles of dress (heavy three piece Harris Tweed suit) and walking was very much akin to that of a farmer. It was good to see everyone relaxed and enjoying the party mood. However, one year was not to my liking when a waitress appeared with starters on each arm and began to serve the person on my right. In doing so I smelt and felt hot oxtail soup being spilt onto my suit from one of dishes she had on her left arm. Although I received an apology from the manager and an undertaking to pay for my suit to be dry cleaned, it was only the second time I had worn the suit and I had dressed to impress the girl who worked at the other end of the office. The suit was never the same afterwards. The manager fulfilled his promise and compensated me for the cleaning. The girl I tried to impress was later transferred to another department and I never saw her again.

Each block either had one or two typing pools each consisting of about ten typists, a mix of copy and shorthand typists. It was while working in this section that I learnt if you really wanted something typed urgently although there were priority and immediate tabs that could be attached to your request, the quickest way was to call for a shorthand typist and pretend to dictate from a written manuscript. The typists got to realise this perhaps because of the fluidness of the dictation but they never complained or made this public, in fact, were pleased to spend time outside their typing pool where otherwise they would most likely be copy typing.

Part way through my time in DNSP, the section moved from E Block along with other sections of DNSP to the newly built J Block, a two storey building built on land between B and C Blocks which didn't please the allotment holders who lost their allotments. They could not complain really as they were allowed to use the land on an ex-gratia free of charge basis. J Block accommodated the whole of the Naval Ship Production organisation with the exceptions of its directing staff which remained in G Block and those in the overseeing service as explained earlier in this chapter.

This move brought the section closer to the pumps specialist section in Block B headed by Commander FE Rudd which meant it was that much easier to go across to the next block and discuss issues face to face rather than using the telephone or by correspondence. It was common practice for Dickie Westcombe to liaise with the Ship Maintenance Authority at Portsmouth Naval Base on issues relating to pumps.

In the December of 1973 the Conservative Government lead by Mr Ted Heath introduced certain measures in an attempt to conserve electricity, one of which was the Three Day Working Week. The period lasted from January to early March 1974 during which commercial users, with certain exceptions, of electricity were allowed to work for three specified consecutive days only each week and not permitted to extend the working day on those days. This measure was brought about because of industrial action by coal miners. I remember on working days we were issued with candles during the late afternoons when it became dark.

Strike action escalated especially in the mining industry. Some readers may recall commotions with disgruntled miners and the police who were there to control picket lines – policemen's helmets were rolling around everywhere and several injuries were sustained on both sides.

Mr Heath, thinking the public would be against the pay dispute with the miners and powers of the unions and therefore would be supportive of the Conservative Party, called a general election. After a period of 'hung parliament' the second general election resulted in a win for the Labour Party and the return of Harold Wilson as Prime Minister.

The new Labour government increased miners' wages by over 30 per cent and a further increase by a similar percentage was achieved without any industrial dispute.

As part of the DNSP organisation, a section called the Equipment Progress Information Centre (EPIC) consisting of a number of technical grades and headed by Rupert Snead was just along the corridor from us. The section produced monthly progress reports formulated on information obtained from various sections and other departments. Rupert was a happy go lucky and an extremely efficient person who managed his staff effectively when it came to producing monthly updated equipment delivery schedules. He did not accept fools gladly and in fact could become quite abrupt with people who made decisions without being aware of all the facts.

He had good reason to act in this fashion as he was one of the survivors from the sinking of the 'T' class submarine HMS *Truculent* on 12 January 1950.

With its crew complement of 56 officers and ratings and 18 dockyard workers *Truculent,* having completed her sea trials in the Thames Estuary following a refit and en route to Chatham Dockyard, was in a collision with the Swedish oil tanker *Divina* who was on passage from Purfleet to Ipswich. It was normal practice for civilian dockyard workers to be present on-board HM vessels undergoing sea trials in case they were required to make any adjustments to machinery or repair. Within a few seconds of the collision *Truculent* sank. Most of the crew survived the initial impact and managed to escape but then perished in the freezing conditions. The *Truculent* sank to a depth of some eighty feet and most of the remainder on-board escaped by flooding the submarine and escaping through a hatch to the surface. A total of 65 men lost their lives that night and only 15 men survived, Rupert being one of them. A further four bodies were recovered when the submarine was salvaged some months later. An inquiry into the sinking apportioned 75 per cent blame to the *Truculent* and 25 per cent to *Divina*.

Dickie Westcombe's cousin Monty Stevens was the owner of a top flat racehorse, Raffingora, trained by Bill Marshall. The horse had many wins over six and seven furlongs throughout the late 60s and early 70s and both Dickie and I had several bets following tips passed to Dickie and we ended up in profit.

During my time in the section, Brendan was transferred to Devonport Naval Base to work in the new frigate complex as Production Manager and was replaced by Benjamin Francis and just before I left to go to Director General Weapons Finance Department, in the spring of 1975 Benjamin was replaced by Douglas Chesterfield. I was grateful for the patience Benjamin devoted in teaching me the fundamentals of Critical Path Analysis. This gave me the basics for understanding the methods employed during ship refits.

On leaving the section I was presented with a golf umbrella and a copy of the Oxford Illustrated Dictionary.

I must thank Brendan for inviting me to Devonport Naval Base and showing me around several frigates that were in various stages of refit. Thank you, Brendan.

CHAPTER TEN

WEAPONS

Having been unsuccessful at a number of interview boards for promotion to executive officer it was decided that I needed experience working in other departments and on 17 March 1975 took me from Foxhill across the city to Ensleigh and to the Director General of Weapons (Navy)'s Finance Branch.

My Assistant Director was Grant 'Jock' Tadd who I had worked with when he was Civil Assistant to DG Ships. He welcomed me into his organisation and introduced me to Geoff Epton, the SEO, Donald Bragg, HEO and union representative who I already knew, Keith Tombs, EO, and to Ernest Havesham, CO, who I was to replace. The team worked closely together and had the services of James Parkhouse, Management Accountant available when required. The staff always knew when Geoff arrived in the morning as the first thing heard from his next door office was the sound of his electric razor. It was not long after that he appeared and in his broad Irish accent wished everyone a good morning. Geoff was an ex Irish youth international and we had a common interest albeit Geoff supported Manchester United I guess because of the Irish contingent including George Best and I supported Manchester City.

The branch was divided into two main sections; one covering Development and the other Production of both surface and underwater naval weapons and associated equipment. I worked in the office covering the finance of weapons development projects and mainly entailed formulating and co-ordinating the Navy Weapons Underwater and Surface Development Programme for the annual Navy Estimates and 10 year spread of expenditure known as Long Term Costings (LTC) with the first 4 years being the PESC years. The financial year ran from 1 April to 31 March.

Although I had no real practical skills in arithmetic I knew how to operate a calculator and remembered the advice given by my maths school teacher to always balance tables down and across before moving on.

It seemed a small world; not only had I worked with Jock Tadd before when he was Civil Assistant to Director General Ships, I also knew Donald through his union work at Foxhill which he remained heavily committed to when he moved across to Ensleigh.

Ernest showed me the ropes for my two weeks' handover before he was appointed to the production side of the department. Ken left to join the production finance section within a month of my arrival and was replaced by Micky Joyce. Micky was a timid type of character who had difficulty working under pressure especially when his figure-work did not balance. This was more so when financial returns had to be made to the Materials Co-ordination II Branch at the Empire Hotel by a certain time. It was Mat Co-ord's responsibility to collate inputs from DRP(Ships) and DWRP to form a major part of the Sea Systems VOTE 8 Navy Estimates and LTC and to forward on to the General Finance Department in Whitehall.

As part of a reorganisation of DGW(N), the Director of Weapons Resources and Programmes (DWRP), similar to DRP(Ships) in the Ship Department, incorporated both finance sections and a newly created Weapons Project Group was formed. The Weapons Project Group was responsible for all weapon project submissions to the General Finance Branch and the Central Defence Secretariat DS4 in Whitehall who in turn would refer them on to the Treasury for formal approval.

The actual development work was undertaken by scientific and technical staff at the Director of Underwater Weapons Projects (DUWP) at Portland, Dorset the design of surface weapons by similar staff at the Director of Surface Weapons Projects (DSWP) at Portsdown, Cosham, Hampshire.

It was not long before Micky realised he was not suited to finance and was transferred to another department. I was given a temporary and geographical promotion to EO lasting more than a year.

My time in DGW(N) spanned two financial years 1975/76 and 1976/77. Financial years ran in annual cycles and people said a two-year posting was quite adequate to gain experience, the first year was a learning curve and the second a refresher of the first year that gave full knowledge and awareness of the various stages and timescales of the financial year.

Ministers in association with the Treasury decided annually on the percentage of savings to be achieved for each Government department for the forthcoming financial year.

In the first instance it was the finance department's responsibility to issue input forms to the DUWP and DSWP for each existing and new project contained in the Yellow Book and for each to be costed based on latest information, taking account of current spend and latest forecast of outturn. The finance officers at DUWP and DSWP consulted each project manager for financial input, annotation and return to DWRP(N). The forms would be coordinated and then be forwarded to General Finance Department in Whitehall who then in consultation with the Treasury would respond advising the level of savings departments should achieve.

It was then up to departments to meet their target savings. This was achieved by assessing and prioritising possible savings for each individual project. These were called Scrutiny Meetings and were chaired at director level with the relevant project officer present. In the case of the Navy Weapons Development Programme it was our job to arrange Scrutiny Meetings at DUWP Portland and DSWP Portsdown. It quite often was not an easy decision to undertake; whether to decide to defer or even cancel a project was dependent on the essentiality, progress or otherwise of the project. Consideration also had to be given to whether a project formed an entirely new concept or if it was being designed to counteract the 'enemies' intention. Some meetings became heated with strong arguments being made by both sides but decisions had to be made due to financial constraints put on the department by the Treasury.

Other tasks that fell to me were the annual production of the Programme Element Costings and the Project Information Books for the Navy Weapons Development Projects. Figurework included both intra-mural and extra-mural expenditure.

Programme Element Costing derived from the Navy Estimates which allowed ministers, etc., to know the savings that would be achieved if particular projects were either deferred or cancelled. Unknowing at the time, this system was developed and introduced into the MOD by my cousin Reginald Browning when working in the Treasury as a management accountant.

The Project Information Book is a classified document and provides a description of all surface and underwater weapon projects in the development programme and contains LTC expenditure tables. It was generally referred to as the Blue Book.

I enjoyed my time working with figures but the pressure placed on us to meet deadline dates was enough for me and others to decide two years was sufficient and it was time to move on.

CHAPTER ELEVEN

CONTRACTS ERA

Having now reached almost half way through my Civil Service career assuming, as things were going, that my retirement age would be 60, I gained promotion to Executive Officer (EO) in early April 1977 and was posted to an entirely new department, namely 'Contracts' at Ensleigh. Unknown to me at the time, the final half of my career was to be spent in the Contract's specialisation field. My time working in this field spanned from April 1977 to October 2003.

Although the MOD Procurement Executive was set up in 1971 to form a single acquisitioning organisation for the three military services, the Royal Navy, the British Army and the Royal Air Force by the Rayner Committee, it took a long time for the rationalisation programme to be fully implemented. The Committee was chaired by Derek Rayner who was then the Head of Marks and Spencer. He became the first Chief of Defence Procurement (CDP). The Executive was later headed by Peter Levene and was replaced in the late 90s by the Defence Procurement Agency. Personally I thought that the procurement executive responsibilities could have been extended even further to include common purchases for other government departments such as the prison and the health services, as well as the MOD. Economies of scales would have led to overall savings on government expenditure. I did put forward a proposal through my line management citing toilet rolls and food as prime examples but I heard nothing more. I assumed my proposal failed to reach the right level.

There were several different types of contracts ranging from the simplest being those awarded by competitive tendering to the more complex types of contracts. Wherever possible the Government's first principle is that all contracts should be awarded wherever possible following competitive tendering. This reminded me of the following:

> I remember reading an article involving two brothers in the Victorian days who had each bought a shop in the seaside resort of Bruton-on-Sea on the south coast from their father's inheritance. The shops were situated overlooking the beach. One address was No. 1 West High Street and the other No. 1 East High Street and besides food and beverages both sold buckets and spades, inflatable rings, beach balls, post cards, etc., and each product type priced the same to the nearest penny. When one shop had a good run on a particular type of product the remaining quantity of product were removed from the shelves and customers advised to go to the other shop until both stock levels became the same. This was not exactly a cartel but did ensure that

both shops received a fair share of the marketplace. It also struck me that Mahatma Ghandi's philosophy that the earth provides sufficient to meet mankind's needs but not for mankind's greed was relevant.

Requests to place non-competitive contracts must be closely scrutinised to ensure that competition is not possible. The type most used for procurement of general items of naval stores is undertaken by the competitive tendering procedure. The other types of contracts for Repair, Research and Development, Works, Services and Sales requirements are undertaken using specific types of contracts with their own particular terms and conditions and pricing arrangements. Pricing arrangements for these types of contracts could vary depending on a number of factors, for instance in the case of single tender contracts when the contractor is able to submit a quotation at the outset and could be considered fair and reasonable, or to submit the quotation part-way through or at the end of the contract term, in which case Standard Condition 43, and for Research and Development contracts Standard Condition 53 would apply.

All types of contract are self-explanatory by their nature and each subject to certain government standard terms and conditions and pricing arrangements. Copies of the booklet referenced Form GC/STORES/1 entitled Standard Conditions of Government Contracts for Stores Purchases Contracts were available to all contracts staff that may have a need to ascertain such information. Other methods of procurement are by 'Running Contract' and Local Purchase Order (LPO).

A Running Contract is not a contract in the true sense, but in legal terms a continuing offer by the contractor to supply goods or services. In simple terms, a contract only exists when an order is placed by an authorised Demanding Officer and the contractor's continuing offer is accepted to form a contract.

Obviously, contracts for new build ships, submarines, refits, weapons and other major items of equipment were subject to more complex types of contracts. I would have liked to have served in such a branch but never had the opportunity.

Guidance for contracts staff was contained in 'The Contracts Handbook' of which everyone above the grade of clerical officer was given a copy and held responsible for updating vide amendments.

The collective name given to a large group of staff engaged on contract work was 'Branch' as opposed to 'Section' as in other departments such as DG Ships and DG Weapons (Navy). Each branch was divided into sub-branches; however, the term 'section' was used to describe a small team of contracts staff, within the sub-branch, engaged on the procurement of smaller packages of work. All staff engaged on contract work is ultimately responsible to the Director General of Defence Contracts, a member of the Admiralty Board.

The golden rule applicable to staff working in the contracts branches of the MOD was emphasised by the statement 'Authority to commit the Secretary of State for Defence in contract matters rests solely with the Defence Contracts staff. Furthermore, staff appointed to any contracts branch in the MOD is held personally liable and answerable to the

Government for their actions such as placing contracts in the absence of financial approval being granted.'

Depending on grade each member of staff was given signing powers meaning that the person is allowed to award and sign contracts up to a certain financial value under delegated authority.

A high proportion of purchases were subject to competitive tender. All invitations to tender documents including the few single tenders sent to prospective contractors were despatched by post with an enclosed tender return label which gave the return address, tender reference and the tender return date. White labels were used for competitive tenders and blue labels were used for single tenders. A duty roster was issued each month giving the names of those formulating the tender panel on a weekly basis. The panel consisted of three persons; the chairman at HEO level from the Contracts Department, and two EOs; one from Contracts Department and the other acting as the independent member from a non-contracts department. The tender panel sat at 2 pm each day under strict conditions. All tenders received on site were posted through a large letterbox into a double locked heavy wooden cabinet, known as the Tender Box, the keys being kept in two separate offices. Each key would be collected by a different panel member and in the presence of all three officers the box would be opened and emptied and the occurrence register removed and envelopes and packages marked for return that day were side-lined and the remainder returned to the box. The two EOs then separated the envelopes and packages carrying the same tender reference into piles.

The piles of envelopes/packages were then opened and each page of the tender document and the envelope, or the outside package, was embossed with the stamp signifying that the tender had been properly processed. Each tender page was meticulously inspected and initialled by each member of the panel and any changes whether manually or otherwise were recorded in the occurrence register and each entry signed by the panel. The occurrence register was then returned to the tender box with the embossing stamp, locked and keys returned to their places for safe keeping. It was quite acceptable for tenders to be received by facsimile or over the telephone providing they reached the tender box before the tender panel sat and recorded and marked accordingly. The tenders were then distributed by hand to the relevant contract branches. There were instances when certain tenders consisted of several sizeable packages and unable to be kept in the tender box and alternative arrangements had to be made for safe storage, usually in a storeroom, and on such occasions the tender panel sat for several hours processing the documentation. It was quite possible for tenders to be received late. These were identified and marked accordingly by the panel and it was the responsibility of the senior officer of the branch concerned whether or not late tenders should be considered in the evaluation. Some offers were technically late meaning that they were posted in time but received after the due date. Special rules governed the consideration and acceptance of a late tender. The tender board procedure solved any query or argument that may be raised at a later date.

I found the work was challenging at first as I would have expected to have had more help and advice from senior staff. It was generally accepted that the contracts department was a closed shop and I believe at one time it had its own promotion system. Having been appointed from outside I was initially treated as an outcast by many senior officers. Personally, I thought they were waiting for me to fail in my endeavour to succeed in becoming a fully-fledged contracts officer. The learning curve was quite extensive but with the help of suitable courses I soon found an acceptable level whereby I could speak authoritatively on the basic functions of contract work and in time, to the disappointment of many senior officers, I believe I reached the standard to be a credit to the department which has also been my aim throughout my career.

Furthermore, I also found the work demanding especially not least having to adapt to the many changes in government contracting and procurement policies from the time I first joined up to the time of my retirement. Nothing stood still for long. The work was rewarding and I met many interesting and dedicated people from the commercial world. Despite the unwelcoming attitude I received from many of the 'established' contracts people in my early days, I am pleased to say it turned out to be one of the best areas of work I undertook during the whole of my Civil Service career. Although I did acquire one further promotion to HEO my only regret is that I was not fortunate enough to obtain promotion earlier than I did particularly in the early part of my career as I was marked 'highly recommended' for promotion by my superiors on several occasions. My work entailed contracting for the following range of products and services which I describe in greater detail in this chapter:

- Ferrous Metals and Stainless Steel
- Electric Cable, Telephone Exchanges and associated items
- Mooring Chain, Anchors and Salvage equipment
- Food (1st Spell)
- Ship Chartering
- Market Testing
- Food (2nd Spell)

It was generally thought that contracts officers having experience and knowledge of the various government terms and conditions of government contracting in the procurement field would be capable of undertaking duties purchasing all types of equipment and services. This was not the case as all equipment and services had their own fundamental intricacies which contracting staff had to be aware of. It was not a case of just grouping a batch of requirements together and sending out invitations to tender; if it had been life would have been that much easier and less taxing.

Contract branches had access to the services provided by Dun & Bradstreet (D&B) in order to establish the financial viability of companies both home and abroad. Such information would generally be sourced when in a single tender situation the contracts branch were unable to assess one way or another whether a particular company was in a financially stable position to fulfil a contract to a specific value. Quite often the advice received from D&B was for the company to obtain and provide the contract branch with a Banker's Performance Guarantee to the value of the intended contract at the outset.

Ferrous Metals and Stainless Steel

My introduction to the contracts field took place on 18 April 1977 when I was posted to the Directorate of Contracts/Supplies and Equipment (DofC/SE). The Directorate's responsibilities covered the purchase of items of general naval stores of various descriptions and my terms of reference covered the procurement of ferrous metals including stainless steel, initially for the Navy but extended a year or so later to cover the requirements also for both the Army and the Royal Air Force in accordance with the Defence rationalisation programme.

Although originally the directorate was set up to procure items of general naval stores over the years it was subject to various changes and re-organisations resulting in a much wider remit. Although I had had some previous involvement with contracts on the main contract with G & J Weir for the repair of pumps, the work I was about to do was nothing in comparison.

The branch was divided into two sub branches; the other branch purchased non-ferrous metals.

By way of explanation, ferrous metals includes carbon steel, mild steel, cast and wrought iron and can be described basically as metal that has iron as the main metal in its composition. Metals that do not contain an appreciable amount of iron, such as aluminium, copper, lead, zinc and tin are known as non-ferrous metals.

The branch, of which my section only formed a part, and headed by a Senior Executive Officer (SEO) was divided into a number of sub-sections each managed by a Higher Executive Officer (HEO) and these were in turn split into further sub-sections headed by an Executive Officer (EO) and each supported by a number of Clerical Officers (COs). The SEO reported to an Assistant Director who in turn reported to the Director.

My SEO was Leon Farmer and was seldom seen outside his ivory castle. The HEO was Veronica Stebbins a spinster in her late 50s/early 60s and a heavy smoker who spent many hours of the day sat at her desk with an empty in-tray and full ash-tray, staring out of the window puffing away at her cigarette and making strange faces. Whether she was concentrating on work or the facial expressions were a habit or aimed at someone in the office opposite no one knew. Having been in contracts since the year dot she was very experienced in this field of work recalling special and legal examples at will. She would appear about 9.30 am each morning and having taken off her coat went straight to the ladies to re-adjust her loose fitting bouffant styled wig. On some occasions it was difficult to control ourselves when she arrived in the office with her wig at right angles caused by the high winds that blew across the open grounds of Ensleigh. We never understood why she did not go to the ladies before coming to the office.

I had a staff of three young clerical officers; Ivor Fletcher, Irwin Cartwright and Peter Richman and when I arrived I noticed that they had their own personally referenced forms and system of operating. This I soon found out was not in accordance with standard practice although on the surface could not be seen as being detrimental to fair competition. However, after a short time I realised that they had their favourites whereby some contractors were being invited to tender on a much regular basis than others even if they had not been successful or competitive for the last purchase. The rules of competitive tendering being that the tender list consisted usually of no more than seven or eight contractors chosen from the Defence Contractors List (DCL), who were either lowest, second or third lowest in price for the previous purchase plus several contractors who had not been invited for some time. The clerical staff should have operated this rotation system. I insisted on approving all future invitations to tenders.

It was common practice for visiting representatives to invite staff out for lunch. With what was going on I could understand the saying 'there were no free lunches'. I could not understand why this had not been recognised and frowned on earlier especially by my predecessor or by Veronica Stebbins. Perhaps they did but chose to ignore. Personally, I had no objection to being invited out for lunch providing everything leading up to the contract awards was above board. However, it became policy for such invites to be recorded in a newly introduced 'Hospitality Book' and this eventually reduced the number of lunches that were accepted.

Procurement of metals came in many forms; plate, sheet and bars of various shapes, all produced to strict Ministry specifications or commercial British Standards.

This was a real eye opener to me as I realised I was spending tax payers money at the stroke of a pen.

At that time I was one of the very few outsiders who entered the contracts arena as an executive officer. Previous to that the contracts department had its own promotion pool and promotions were made from within – a ringed fenced arrangement. This was eventually abolished and subsumed into a general promotion system run by Civil Establishment Branch II list, and promotion opportunities became open on a nationwide basis. It took quite a while for me to be accepted although some senior officers were reluctant to accept the change of situation and others never really did, thinking that 'contracts' was a specialised field and that contracts staff was an elite brand and no one else could do the work. I agree it is a specialised field but I and the other few recent new appointees proved that people from other backgrounds were quiet capable of performing the duties of the grade providing the necessary training was given.

The standard procedure for handling financially approved requisitions in DofC/SE, for general naval store items received from Director of Store and Transport (Navy), DGST(N) in Block D was in the case of my sub-section for the clerical officers to first log in the requisitions and categorise them into individual packages for each type of equipment appropriate to specification. Once the number of requisitions for the same type of ferrous metals taking into account the contract and delivery lead times had reached a sizeable number and value, invitations to tender were prepared and issued to prospective tenderers for return by a specified date. This included items that were sourced through competition and single tender. Once received, via the tender board, tenders were evaluated by the clerical officers and a proposal on item allocation based on lowest acceptable price meeting technical requirements was referred to senior staff for scrutiny and approval. Following approval, formal contract documents were drawn up and passed to the appropriate line manager for signature and then despatched and copies of which were distributed to the relevant requisition issuing DGST(N) branch and the relevant overseeing areas, technical authorities, store depot and the accounts department in Liverpool with the distribution sheet identifying by reference to the requisitions and line items. The registered file was endorsed accordingly.

A real bug bear to all contracts staff that purchased items of general naval stores was the monthly Provisioning Review Statements (PRS) undertaken by the requisitioning department, of Director General Stores and Transport (DGST(N)). These computerised statements providing listings of literally thousands of requisitions under product Class Groups and NATO stock numbers detailing item description, quantities required, delivery dates and specifications that were sent to the contracts sections for procurement action. Allowances were built-in to cover the necessary lead times for tendering, manufacture and delivery in order to maintain the required levels of stock in store. This first computer run could not be relied upon as being an accurate statement because of the lack of confidence on the DGST(N) branch responsible for updating records. It should have been a simple but painstaking task for the branch to update the computer record as soon as it had received a copy of the contract or the invitation to tender. This meant that DGST(N) referred the tabulations to the contract sections to be updated and returned so that the central computer data could be revised, before a second run was made. Despite this, I still found many a time that the second shorter tabulated version still included requisitions that had been placed on contract. It is said that the computer is only as good as the data put in. How true this is. It was evident without control; the system resulted in excess stock. After months and months of complaining management realised that to review the first run was taking too much of contracts staffs' time and a decision was made to undertake one PRS each month with instructions given for the updating section to be more thorough. This left contracts staff to concentrate on their proper work.

All requirements for ferrous metals, except for single tender sourced proprietary items such special submarine 'T' sections and QT35 materials which were ordered direct from British Steel Corporation works at Darlington, were awarded following competition. All metals were consigned to store for eventual issue to HM Naval Bases for ships and submarines undergoing refit or repair.

Our main contractors were both manufacturers such as the British Steel Corporation, Darlington Simpson Rolling Mills and Sheffield Forgemasters and stockists including Walkersteel, GKN, Aviation Metals, AALCO and Cashmore Stainless.

Thinking of starting a rumpus and unknowing to me Ivor Fletcher and Irwin Cartwright concocted a situation by sending a cheque in a brown envelope supposedly from a Ministry contractor to themselves. The envelope was discovered in transit and the matter was brought to the attention of senior officers and eventually referred to the Ministry of Defence Police. Both Ivor and Irwin were interviewed separately by the police and Ministry security staff and each gave written statements and were warned that they may hear further. Several days passed without hearing anything and both lads became concerned that the prank had escalated to a high level and had backfired on them and more importantly were worried about losing their jobs. After a few more days the police called for them and each were given a severe telling off and returned to office highly embarrassed with their tails between their legs. They fortunately kept their jobs. I was far from pleased as it gave other people the impression I had little or no control over my staff. This was a stupid prank to play and I told them so in no uncertain terms. I am pleased to say that Ivor and Irvin learnt their lesson and caused me no further embarrassment from that point on, in fact the standard of their work improved immensely.

Peter Richman was a quiet and unobtrusive person who performed his duties effectively with little involvement needed from me and who I was pleased to have as a member of my staff.

Time passed by, Veronica Stebbins retired and after some re-organisational changes I saw my duties increase with my responsibilities now covering the procurement of all ferrous and non-ferrous metals for all three service departments. There was no additional staff allocated to undertake this extra work.

At the invitation of British Steel Corporation I visited their Llanwern Steelworks, South Wales with Byron Teddington, a much older person than me, who was then my Assistant Director. We were shown the whole steel making process from first acquiring the right mixes of materials, heating liquid metal to correct temperature in massive ladles and after taking samples for laboratory testing, pouring to produce very large slabs which are then elongated to further produce steel bars or rolled to produce steel plate and sheets. The process was called continuous casting. I was surprised at the small number of workers in the steel works. There could not be any more than a dozen or so workers visible during our visit and many of them were sat in front of monitors. I could now understand why the workers went out on strike so often knowing that their jobs were at risk with the introduction of the automated continuous casting operation which put British steel production on an equal footing with foreign competition.

The visit entailed climbing up and along high gantries in order to get to better observation points. This had an effect on Byron as we learned he had overnight suffered a heart attack. Knowing that Byron was likely to be away from work for some time resulted in staff under him being promoted to the next level on a temporary and geographical basis, until he returned to office. Thankfully Byron made a good recovery and returned to work with no lasting effects and all other staff reverted to their normal grades.

Some months later leaving the office at the end of a working day, a group of us found Byron standing by his car in what was known as the sunken car park, an overflow of the main car park. He said that he was having problems starting and the engine would not turn over and thought it may be due to the battery being flat. With Brian sat in the driver's seat, four of us pushed the car up and down the slope with Byron at the controls. The car would not start and it was realised after the fourth attempt that Byron had not switched on the ignition. After the fifth attempt with sweat pouring from each of us some appropriate but not nice words were expressed as Byron disappeared into the distance.

Byron was an inoffensive person who was popular with his staff and with his wide knowledge of experience in the contracts world always had the time to provide valid reasons for his decision making. Besides seeing Byron regularly as work required the only time we had seen our directors and above was at Christmas time when they did their annual round wishing the staff seasonal greetings. On another occasion I could hear footsteps follow me in the corridor so approaching a closed swing door I politely held the door open and the gentleman passed through without even a thank you. It turned out be one of my directors. He did not know me from Adam; I felt like introducing myself but decided not to. On reflection I wish I had as it may have caused him some embarrassment or perhaps I should have let the door swing back on him.

The following photographs show parts of the steel making process and the diagram provides a simple guide of the complete process.

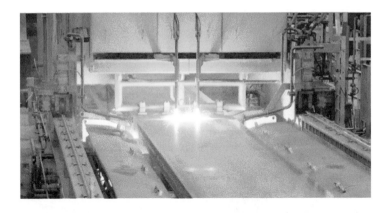

Steel making process

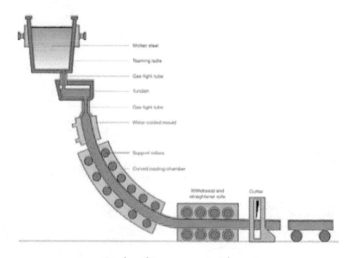

Steel making process guide

Electric Cable, Telephone Exchanges and associated equipment

From the procurement of metals branch I moved to another contract branch within the same directorate this time responsible for the purchase of electric cable and telephone exchanges and associated equipment.

Again all contracts for electric cable were subject to competitive tendering with Sterling, BICC, AEI and Pirelli being the main contractors. Telephone exchanges, usually System X, and ancillary equipment mainly required at Ministry establishments were awarded to Standard Telephones and Cables Ltd following single tender action.

The branch was headed by Terry Caldwell, (SEO), with Evan Purdon as HEO. Both were very keen bowls players, turning out regularly in their whites (both indoors and outdoors) for the Civil Service Bowls Club team. I was supported by two clerical officers, these being Brenda Holt and Adam Harman. Both were new to contracts and took up the reigns enthusiastically to become independent and reliable officers. The other half of the branch was led by Jill Harrington (EO) and two clerical officers including Jim Miller. Jim was a keen golfer and I introduced him to my club, Tracy Park GC and he went on to become a real golfing talent and in no time at all became the club champion.

As explained earlier those new to the contracts field were not welcomed with open arms and were inclined to be treated as some kind of dimwit. I recall having to go and discuss a particular contract issue with Terry Caldwell taking Brenda with me who gave a comprehensive verbal brief. I was astonished that despite the excellent brief she gave he read the file from cover to cover not really taking any notice of the briefing in fact asking questions on matters that were adequately covered by Brenda in her briefing. This session took twice as long as I would have expected as it would appear the SEO had time on his hands, unlike his supporting staff.

Another occasion tickets were issued for the Royal Naval Equipment Exhibition (RNEE) at Whale Island near Portsmouth. The tickets were limited and names were drawn out of a hat and Terry Caldwell and I were the only ones successful in the branch. We travelled together by coach from Ensleigh and chatted in general terms on the journey down south. Whilst going round the exhibition we were approached by a group from DG Ships. Unknowing that I knew the group having previously worked as its section clerk some years earlier, Terry Caldwell introduced them to me as Ron Thomson and everyone in the group including myself turned around looking for this person. At least he got my initials right. I grinned at the group and shrugged my shoulders. Surely, he should have at least got my name right as I was one of only five executive officers that reported to him. I think Ron Thomson must have worked in the contracts department donkey's years earlier when everyone knew each other and the department was like one big family. At this point I seriously considered whether I had made the right decision to move to the contracts area especially as my second reporting officer did not recognise me by name. As time went by many of the old established staff retired and were replaced by outsiders and the attitude that prevailed gradually changed for the better and the newcomers soon outnumbered the remainder which to my mind was a good thing.

Although there were pot plants on the window shelves I thought the office needed something more in line with latest trends so I bought a small aquarium and a goldfish which was put in a prime position in the office. We named the goldfish 'Bob' for obvious reasons. A kind word and the guards agreed to feed the goldfish at weekends and holiday times.

It was whilst working in this branch that the European Council Supplies Directive 77/62/EEC dated 21 December 1976, on the procurement of goods, applicable to all UK government and local authorities became operational in the

Ministry of Defence. The Directive changed the policy by which the MOD went about procuring its equipment. All new non-warlike requirements over the financial threshold equivalent to 200,000 euros had first to be advertised in the European Community Official Journal (EC/OJ). The Journal was published in all languages of the countries in the European Community affording the opportunity to all companies in the member states to request to be included on the tender list for the specified requirement. Each response showing an interest had to be accompanied with a set of the latest audited accounts, which would be examined by Ministry accountants to establish financial viability if the company was in contention to be awarded the contract.

Being in the MOD it was often difficult to differentiate which items were non-warlike and those which were warlike. Obviously a weapon like a torpedo or missile was warlike but how about a reel of electric cable manufactured to a Ministry and not a commercial specification. There were strict rules and procedures associated with the Directive such as a group of requisitions for similar items of equipment with values less than the 200,000 euro threshold could not be handled individually. The Directive prolonged the whole procurement cycle and major adjustment had to be made to accord with the extended contracting lead-time.

In 1978/79 the country experienced what became known as the Winter of Discontent. The Labour Prime Minister at the time was James Callaghan and during the coldest winter for many years widespread strikes by the public sector were organised by the trade unions demanding higher pay rises and, in particular, against the Government's imposed rule for public sector workers' pay rises to be kept below five per cent. Trade Unions held several 24-hour strikes. I was in two minds whether to take part in strike action; on one hand I was a staunch supporter of the Labour Party and on the other hand I was also a strong believer in trade unionism. After some agonising consideration I decided to go on strike. I went on strike for a total of three days and had my pay deducted for my unauthorised absences.

Dates were selected by the trade union on a localised basis and establishments in Bath and nationwide were picketed. Television and the local press were busy interviewing trade union officials. It did not help matters as the weather turned very cold in the early months of 1979 with blizzards and deep snow rendering some jobs impossible, reducing retail spending and worsening the economy. Also many roads were impassable and refuse collection stopped as collectors went on strike and local ancillary workers in the National Health Service formed picket lines to blockade hospital entrances resulting in many hospitals reduced to accepting emergency patients only. Those who, because of weather conditions, were unable to reach their place of work were instructed to go to the nearest public service offices where work would be found.

Furthermore, in an attempt to curb excessive wage demands, the Government imposed a ruling on defence contractors that before receiving a contract they had to first sign, at company secretary level, a declaration of undertaking that they, and their sub-contractors, would not award pay increases to their employees above the Government's guideline.

The more militant strikers were those based at the Defence Bill Paying Department in Liverpool. When not taking strike action they worked to rule. This created problems for the Government as its Defence contractors could not be guaranteed to be paid on their nominated day of the month under the DAB10 procedure. In an attempt to overcome the problem the Government set up temporary offices up and down the UK so that contractors could go in person and collect payment against certified certification. Although this helped it did not alleviate the problem as many contractors suffered from having cash-flow issues to contend with.

Weather conditions subsided and Brenda, Adam and I were invited to the Colston Hall, Bristol by one of the Ministry's contractors to listen to the Farraday Lecture being given on fibre optic cable and the science behind its development. Although technically, most of the contents of the lecture went over our heads we did pick up on certain basic information and the intended future use of fibre optics.

One morning when Brenda and I arrived in the car park at the same time I noticed that smoke was coming from underneath her car's bonnet and in no time had turned into a raging fire. Luckily Brenda had parked away from other vehicles and managed to get out of the car in time and the fire brigade was called. This attracted a large crowd and in the meantime a quick thinking person arrived from the block with a fire extinguisher and doused the fire. The fire brigade arrived soon after with siren blaring. The vehicle was eventually towed away and it was some weeks later before Brenda bought a replacement.

A black cloud came over the department when it was announced that Jill Harrington who had been absent on sick leave had died of cancer. She was a spinster in her mid-30s and a very pleasant person who was an active member of the local historical group and loved dressing up appropriately to act out historical battles. Jill is sadly missed by her friends and colleagues. Her sudden passing affected the office for several months to come.

Martin Weldon filled the post vacated by Jill. The young lads in the office, Archie Hill and Jim Miller who worked at the other end of the office got up to some pranks. Martin Weldon lived out in the country and made it known that he was terrified of mice. His house backed onto fields and field mice often came into his house and had to be removed by his wife before being killed by the cat and presented to Martin as a gift. With this in mind Archie Hill brought in a toy furry mouse and when Martin went out of the office he put the mouse in his lunchbox under a lettuce leaf. Lunchtime came and Martin as usual reached forward for his lunchbox and as he removed the lid and saw the toy mouse he jumped backwards from his chair which crashed into the wall behind him and he gave out one almighty scream. It took him quite a few minutes to recover.

On another occasion Martin and Archie and I were standing at a four-drawer filing cabinet discussing a particular contract when Archie quietly left the group and put on a prosthetic face mask of a very aged man and returned to the group unnoticed by Martin. A minute or so passed before Martin looked up from the contract document and turned round to Archie asking for his opinion. Seeing the mask Archie was wearing Martin jump a foot in the air falling backwards against the office wall holding his chest. All good harmless fun and Martin had no lasting effects.

It came to our knowledge that he was also a hoarder who would never throw anything away without being certain that containers were completely empty. Before he left for work he would look in the dustbin and retrieve any packages put there by his wife that he thought were not completely emptied and would put them in the garage to be inspected on his return from work. This included toothpaste tubes, butter cartons and washing up liquid bottles. His wife next day would find them returned to their position in the house. I would like to have called him something else rather than a hoarder. Martin was also a keen footballer playing in defence for the Civil Service. He continued playing well into his forties.

A feat I will always remember was at the time when office staff undertook their annual task of re-arranging office files, moving some to archives and the storeroom and others from one cabinet to another. Andy and Jim, both about 5'10' tall and of average build decided to put on a circus act by diving through a 18'x16' metal frame which held suspended files in place. I held the frame at shoulder height and each with a run up dived arms outstretched through the frame without touching the sides and ending up with a forward roll on the office carpet.

Both could easily have been gymnasts in the circus.

Some years later in 1984, the Government Communications Headquarters (GCHQ) at Cheltenham was the centre of a political row when the Conservative Government of Margaret Thatcher prohibited its employees from belonging to a trade union. It was claimed that joining a union would be in conflict with national security. A number of mass national one-day strikes were held to protest against this decision, seen as another step to wider bans on trade unions. This caused a lot of bad feeling between union members and the Conservative Government. Appeals to British Courts and the European Commission of Human Rights were unsuccessful. The Government even offered a sum of money to each employee who agreed to give up their union membership.

The ban was eventually lifted in 1997 by the incoming Labour Government, with a part of the Public and Commercial Services Union (PCS) being formed to represent the interests of all employees at all grades. In 2000, a group of 14 former GCHQ employees, who had been dismissed after refusing to give up their union membership, were offered re-employment, which only a few accepted.

Mooring Chain, Anchors and Salvage equipment

After spending three years procuring electric cable I moved offices and became responsible for the procurement of anchors, mooring chain, steel wire rope, sinkers, fenders and salvage equipment often referred to as the heavy end of naval equipment. This appointment took me on visits to commercial manufacturers mainly in the black-country.

With Richard Thomas as my SEO and with one of his three sub-sections headed by Jack Gillingham as the HEO, and Marion Rundle, Hazel Britain, Christopher Roberts, Granville Morgan and Stewart Wainwright being the clerical officers, supporting me as the EO.

Marion, Hazel and Granville had been working in the office well before I arrived and were all experienced and efficient at their jobs. Stewart and Christopher were relatively new. Stewart joined the Ministry having served as a rating in the Royal Navy until he was retired on medical grounds due to a leg injury and within no time at all he quickly mastered his duties. However, he had an annoying habit that once he completed a task he would reach for a paperback and start reading instead of going to his in-tray for his next job. He would not work under his own initiative but waited to be told to do so. It took him quite a time to adapt to this way of working. I think this stemmed from his days in the Royal Navy where it was generally accepted one a job was done you waited to be told what to do the next. I am glad to say that Stewart did eventually comply with the recognised procedures.

Of all the clerical officers that came to work for me there was only one that stood head and shoulders above the rest. That person was Christopher Roberts who dealt with his contractors in a confident manner, his worked was concise and faultless and I am pleased to say that he went on to gain promotion to several higher grades moving on to Army Land Command Headquarters at Andover where I unfortunately lost contact with him.

Staff wise it was a happy office to work in. Jack Gillingham would be inclined to keep a low profile, delegating as much work as possible and invariably pass on a proposal to senior officers without commenting, only to write 'Agree with proposal', hence relying on the information put forward by his staff as correct. His wife ran an old people's care home which I believe they eventually bought and moved to so Jack had other things to occupy his mind and was not dependent on just his Civil Service salary. Jack took early retirement and was replaced by Daniel Bromington who originated from Weymouth and had previously worked in the prison service. Marion and Granville were experienced in contract work and could be relied upon to do their work in an organised and methodical manner and needed no guidance from me. Marion could speak Mandarin and was on the MOD's list of translators and was asked from time to time to convert Chinese into English for which she received payment.

Granville's outside interest was model soldiers and he would set out his model soldiers to re-enact historic battle scenes following accounts he had read in books. His father was a member of the clergy and I recall Granville telling me his elderly father was becoming very absent minded and would often leave the house wearing two hats, one on top of the other which amused the congregation. Unknown to us at the time Granville had a female penfriend in Madagascar and Granville, having applied for two weeks' leave flew to out to visit his penfriend. He did not return to work on the day he should have and after a couple of days had passed he contacted the department for an extension to his leave which was granted. No one knew at the time that he was in Madagascar or the reason for his request for extended leave. It transpired that Granville needed this extra time to make the necessary arrangements with the appropriate authorities for his lady friend who was now more than just a penfriend to come and live with him in England. Granville returned to work and within a short time he and his friend were reunited in Bath and they married and soon began a family.

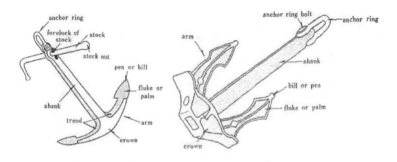

The 'Admiralty' design Anchor   The Byers 'stockless' Anchor

The Ministry had its recognised approved suppliers of anchors and chain which was purchased by means of competition. To understand the manufacturing process and to see such items at first hand we accepted several invites from various contractors and were given conducted tours of their factories where each operation was explained in detail. This was most helpful when it came to describing particular types of products.

My work brought me into regular contact with Frank Merrick, Chief Mooring and Salvage Officer and his staff Clive

Jackman and Jack Cope in the organisation of the Director of
Marine Services (DMS(N)). Marine Services being responsible
for salvage work and associated equipment. Frank also carried
the title of the Government's Chief Salvage and Mooring Officer
(SALMO) and was called on in times of crisis and emergencies
at sea involving vessels and aircraft.

Stud link chain cable

The Ministry's contractors manufactured all its chain requirements to imperial measurements; there was no exact metric equivalent for chain manufacture undertaken on the continent or elsewhere. In accordance with recently introduced EC Procurement rules the next requirement covering new manufacture imperial size chain cable had to be advertised in the European Union/Official Journal EC/OJ. As a result the most attractive offer received price-wise was submitted by a Spanish company based in Bilbao. However doubt existed at the technical assessment stage over whether the mooring chain being offered was fully compliant to the imperial Ministry specification even allowing for acceptable manufacturing tolerances. The Spanish company was insistent that their product was capable of fulfilling the Ministry's requirements.

As the department needed sound grounds for rejecting such an offer it was agreed that I should accompany Clive Jackman from DMS(N) and Gregory Fish, from the cable specialist section, on an visit to Spain to verify or otherwise the company's claim of suitability of their chain. We met with the directors of the company and after lengthy and detailed discussion and examination of sample cable and viewing their process facilities, it was decided that the company's offer was technically acceptable. A statement to this effect being signed by both the company directors and the MOD technical representative, with provisos to safeguard Ministry interests and I proceeded to write the contract. Whilst we had to comply with EC contract rules, imperial vs. metric caused many problems especially when it concerned dimensions.

We travelled back from Bilbao on 25 January 1990 and experienced the tail end of what became known as the Burns Day Storm and was described as one of the worst storms to hit the UK in the last 50 years. The return flight from Bilbao was uneventful until we were coming in to land at Heathrow. The aircraft was buffeted so much that it landed at a different terminal and we waited several hours on-board the aircraft until we were bussed to our scheduled arrival point. There was little information from the flight deck as to the extent of the storm, which had apparently at one point reached hurricane force and we did not realise the extent of the wind force until the crew opened the rear door for passengers to disembark for transfer to our proper terminal. All papers were torn out of passenger's hands and blown to the forward bulkhead as if someone had decided to crazy wallpaper with a mixture of newspapers and magazines.

Once back at our schedule terminal we made our way to the Hertz office to pick up our hire car. The journey along the M4 back to Bath took over four hours as we were travelling very slowly and bumper to bumper. As we arrived in Bath in the early hours of the morning we noticed that a balustrade had been blown off a house in the Paragon but it was not until the next morning that we knew about the amount of damage caused by the storm. I did not realise the seriousness of the storm until I read in next day's newspaper and saw the TV news that the storm was responsible for the deaths of 47 people in England and the actor Gordon Kaye who appeared in the popular TV series *'Allo 'Allo!* suffered serious head injuries when he was hit by an advertising hording.

With the Ministry it was a gradual change to metric measurement and that was mainly on new equipment. It would have been an unaffordable proposition to change all existing equipment to align with metric standards.

Another unfortunate case was the contract placed with a Belgian company who had responded to the EC/OJ advert for the supply of mooring chain cable which was manufactured to the required specification. The outcome being when the chain was delivered to Portsmouth Naval Base it was found that the company had delivered second-hand chain painted to look like new. During the supply process I requested through my line management that I should visit Belgium with technical staff to ensure the contractor had met the Ministry's requirements prior to despatch to the UK. The request was based on the problem previously experienced with the Spanish manufactured chain. My request was rejected as the contract invoked STANAG, the NATO reciprocal agreement, as did the contract placed with the Spanish company. The STANAG procedure placed full responsibility for inspection on the relevant quality authority of the country undertaking the contract. I could foresee this escalating to a country vs. country dispute from one of a contractual nature. Fortunately the cable supplied had been manufactured to imperial dimensions but neither the company nor the Belgian inspectorate failed to understand that the specification called for 'new' manufacture so it was non-compliant. The Belgian contractor was instructed to collect the chain by a certain date otherwise the chain would be disposed to the best advantage of the Crown. The dispute remained ongoing and was never resolved while I was in post.

Perhaps one of the most interesting and responsible roles I undertook was to issue a single tender for the design and manufacture and trialling of a Single Point Mooring (SPM) buoy required for use by the Army Department. There were sound grounds for going to single tender. DMS(N) was the technical authority and Jim Cope was the project manager for the project. As the use of the buoy when deployed was classified the product was categorised as 'warlike' and was therefore exempt from EC rules governing competition.

Besides keeping my assistant director abreast of progress I was basically left to oversee the contract through its entirety. After technical and financial evaluations approval was given to award the contract to a renowned manufacturer of single point moorings. As the value of the contract (£1.5m) exceeded my delegated signing powers the contract was signed by the assistant director. Although I had to pass all proposals in writing through my line management none made any comments other than sign off their names before passing to the assistant director for approval. On completion of manufacture the anchor handling vessel *Maersk Reader* was chartered by the MOD and the buoy was transported by road and delivered to Burntisland for trialling in the Firth of Forth.

As the deployment stage was priced on the basis of actual costs it was agreed that I should be present on-board the hired flat bottom work boat with wheelhouse and small galley to observe and witness the deployment and trialling stages for pricing purposes. In order to do this I travelled on the night sleeper from Bristol to Edinburgh and by bus on to Leven and Methil to find my pre-booked guest house. Jim and an officer from the Army department had travelled to Scotland the day before to arrange the preliminaries and remained on-board *Mearsk Reader* throughout the deployment. That evening I explored the area only to find in one direction was St Andrews Golf Club and in the other East Fife's football ground; incidentally this was where Chesney Ferris first started his professional football career.

I retired to bed early before joining the observer vessel at 7.30 sharp next morning at Methil docks. This was the agreed time the vessel would sail each morning although one morning the vessel did sail without me due to a misunderstanding. I was left to observe from the Port Master's office using a pair of borrowed binoculars. The *Maersk Reader* left Burntisland on the first day of the trials and remained on station until work for the day had completed and the observer vessel was given instructions to return to Methil. A period of four days was allowed for the trial but with everything going without a hitch it was completed a day early. On returning to Methil later than usual on the third day the skipper called to his deckhand that he was having trouble making progress due to tidal conditions and may have to call for assistance. I had thoughts of the vessel being taken by the tide into the North Sea. The skipper tackled the outgoing tide by approaching the inlet at several angles and with dust drawing near we finally made it to our berth. I did not dwell on this too much only to think to myself thankful that the weather and sea conditions were kind to us throughout the trialling operation. I feared to think if the weather had deteriorated at any time just how the vessel would have coped with such conditions.

I had noticed that there were several certificates pinned to the vessels' inner wall depicting its seaworthiness and safety features. I thought I was a good sailor but this was never proven thankfully. I returned to office and finalised the contract by agreeing a firm price for the trialling of the SPM.

The observer vessel pictured above is similar to the vessel chartered to witness the deployment of the SPM

Food (1st Spell)

My introduction to food supply came in the late 1980s. I first thought that the post would be more suitable to the female gender as it was normal practice for them to do the family's weekly shop and was more conversant with foodstuff and prices than their male counterpart. I soon changed my mind when I began to face the complexities associated with food procurement. The department was then known as the Directorate of Supply Food Management (DSFM) and the contracts cell consisting of Sheila Price (SEO), Rodney Munday (HEO) and myself were responsible for the procurement and management of food supply contracts to the Royal Navy only. The branch had recently been bedded in with Director General Stores and Transport formerly the Director of Victualling. With the advent of rationalisation within the Ministry of Defence and a number of departmental changes a new department was created for the purposes of forming a combined tri-service directorate for the procurement and supply of all food provisions to all ships and submarines and shore establishments of the Royal Navy, Army barracks and training exercises and all Royal Air Force establishments. This is where I first encountered Navy, Army and Air Force Institutes (NAAFI).

NAAFI had a long association with the British Defence forces having been created in 1921 when the Expeditionary Force Canteens (EFC) and the Navy and Army Canteen Board (NACB) were combined to run the recreational establishments needed by the Armed Forces, and to sell goods to their service personnel and their families.

NAAFI expanded its operation over the next 15 or so years, supporting military bases and deployments across the world, from Bermuda and Jamaica, to Singapore and China. At the outbreak of WWII NAAFI grew exponentially to support the troops on active service, with the number of employees rising from 8,000 to a peak of 110,000 and the number of trading outlets growing from 1,350 to nearly 10,000.

In the post war years, NAAFI rescaled its operations, closing canteens at a rate of 200 per week and the number of employees reducing to 65,000 by 1947. From the 1950s onwards, NAAFI has supported the British Forces at home and abroad, including the conflicts in The Falklands, the two Gulf Wars and Afghanistan amongst many others. Today NAAFI operates in far fewer locations but is present in Germany, Gibraltar, Northern Ireland, Brunei, the South Atlantic Islands and on board HM Ships. With around 100 outlets, NAAFI still provides convenience and a 'taste of home' to our forces and their families overseas.

Going back to the 1980s, NAAFI had held the long standing arrangement for food supply to all service establishments home and abroad. Furthermore, a new contractual arrangement was awarded to NAAFI on a single tender basis with the proviso that the requirement would be subject to competition when the three year contract period expired. Soon after being awarded the contract NAAFI's computer system failed which meant everything had to be undertaken manually. This caused a lot of aggravation and it took quite a time to resolve the issue.

Pressure was put on DSM, in particular Sheila and Rodney to draw up a competitive tender package in the shortest time possible. The commodity list covered over twelve hundred items of frozen, chilled, ambient and fresh products and in excess of 300 delivery destination addresses home and abroad.

After advertising the requirement in the EC/OJ and the MOD Contracts Bulletin invitations to tender were issued to a number of companies. The MOD employed the services of various outside independent food specialists including Jill Dennis of *The Grocer* to oversee the tender evaluation stage. After lengthy and exhaustive negotiations the contract was awarded to the contractor offering best value for money. The requirement has since been the subject of further competition between several food suppliers and the resulting contract was awarded to a different contractor again on the basis of best value for money. The contract is known as the MOD's World Wide Food Supply Contract.

My first role in food supply branch covered the procurement of items of food that were produced and consigned by the Contractor to the RN Victualling Depot (RNVD) near Botley in rural Hampshire prior to being sent to Portsmouth Naval Base to be made up into Operational Ration Packs (ORP). In addition my sub-section was responsible for the procurement of provisions for in-flight meals and food supply for Winter Exercises in Norway. Such procurement was by competitive tender and evaluation involved referral of samples to the Food Research Association (CCFRA) at Chipping Camden to establish that food products were strictly in accordance with Ministry of Defence specification. Being the end user service personnel were invited to participate in the taste panel sessions. The evaluation process included establishing the correct calorific levels and proportions of ingredients etc. and taste panels before an offer, if any, was deemed acceptable. An award of contract was made on the basis of the best value for money. It was not always the case to accept the lowest priced offer. As people's taste vary from person to person and samples were considered acceptable to some and not others, contracts were more often than not awarded on a majority points assessment basis. Selection was subjective.

At the first progress meeting I attended at RNVD, it was explained that the stone built corrugated roof store on the outskirts of the land was often invaded by squirrels from the neighbouring woods despite pest control efforts. This was a continuing problem; not least the expense of disposing of possibly contaminated food as the rations were only stored in cardboard boxes and easily assessable by squirrels. At the meeting I came up with an innovative suggestion that the problem might be resolved if several large piles of nuts were to be left outside the ten foot high perimeter fence which would keep the squirrels occupied and stop them entering the storage areas. The chairman frowned at me when I made this suggestion as though I had just come out of the loony bin. I wondered, was this because I was a newcomer and no one else had suggested this knowing that the problem had been on-going for months? My suggestion was never implemented and food continued to be written off. For the sake of 50 pounds or so worth of hazel nuts I thought the saving in write-offs would have avoided mounting disposal costs of thousands of pounds over a relatively short period of time until such time a more permanent remedy was found.

Exercises in Norway included the presence of Special Forces and therefore specific arrangement had to be made. The contractor received special instructions to deliver food rations to particular drop-off points out in the wilds identified only by map grid references for collection by the elite forces so that their whereabouts were kept secret without being compromised.

The procurement of in-flight meals for RAF flights followed the same procedure as was used for ORP.

Besides doing our day to day work all EO grades in the Directorate took their turn as Secretary to the DGST(N) Management Board meetings. The board chaired by a Grade 5 head of department consisted of six directors and the secretary whose duties included issue of agendas and taking the minutes. Meetings were held monthly. When my turn came, an item on the agenda was left blank. When we came to this item I was surprised when I was asked to leave the room temporarily as a staff matter was to be discussed. Because of its nature the subject had to be treated in strict confidence. On leaving the room I felt like informing the chairman that I had been positively vetted to a high level which probably others present had not. Wishing not to be seen as objective I left the room and returned when called. The minute for this item was left blank. The meetings usually lasted the morning and because there were about a dozen of us the secretary's duties did not affect our normal duties. I left food procurement with a different attitude and outlook to when I started.

Ship Chartering

It was time to move on again. I transferred to the Directorate of Contracts branch responsible for ship chartering which included Ships Taken Up From Trade, (STUFT) and the contracting of certain operations involving marine services. The branch consisted of Richard Brooks (SEO), Sheila Price (HEO) – who had earlier moved from food supply, me (EO) and Dick Westcombe (CO) under and reporting to Percy Fielding, the AD Contracts. Dick had been in the branch for many years and was the fountain of all knowledge relating to ship chartering with the work of the branch and I am particularly grateful for the advice and guidance he gave me in the early weeks and months. The department already had a number of vessels on charter which included two vessels stationed in the Falkland Islands; the tug *Indomitable* chartered from Alexandra Towing Ltd, and the anchor handling vessel *Oil Mariner* from Oil Ltd.

A charter party is a contract agreed between the ship owner and the customer, in our case the Ministry of Defence. There are a number of different types of charter party, the most common being 'time' where the customer hires the vessel manned and operated by the owner for a specified period of time at agreed daily rates and 'bareboat' charter where the owner of the vessel hands over the operation of that vessel to the customer for him to man and operate as if he owned it for period of time at an agreed daily rate. This work entailed meeting such requirements received from various government departments such as the Hydrographic and Meteorological departments and the MOD itself, particularly DG Ships and the Director of Marine Services (Naval). Vessels chartered for the Hydrographic Department to undertake survey work were manned by Royal Navy personnel referred to as Naval Parties. Survey work resulted in the production of ordnance maps of the sea both coastal and oceanic. Obviously, work undertaken for the Met Office was required for weather forecasting purposes.

It was my task once receiving schedule of requirements detailing the type and details of vessel and the type of charter required, to write to Mr Reginald Bolton, the Government Freight Market Representative at the Baltic Exchange, St Mary Axe, London advising him of the requirements and for him to obtain offers from the floor of the Exchange and to report back to me.

At the invitation of Reginald Bolton I visited the Baltic Exchange and was given a tour of the building which I found most interesting especially the way trading took place on the floor usually finalised by a handshake. The Baltic was severely damaged by an IRA bomb in 1992.

With the HEO being transferred back to food procurement and the post awaiting a replacement I was given temporary promotion to fill the vacant position. It was decided not to fill the post I vacated so I ended up doing both jobs. I must stress that Dick did extremely well accepting extra duties and although he did not benefit financially appropriate comments were made in his annual staff report. I honestly believed he was that content working in this field and to have been moved on promotion would have been a disappointment to him despite the extra pay.

Within a day or so of beginning my new duties as a HEO

and with the SEO out of office I received a telephone call from a Captain RN working in the Directorate of Naval Plans, Main Building, Whitehall and after first asking for my status advised me that the Prime Minister had given instructions for the Ministry of Defence to urgently source a replacement vessel for HMS *Endurance* who was apparently nearing the end of her seaworthiness for service in the South Atlantic.

The meeting was hastily arranged for the next day in the main conference room, Old Admiralty Building, Whitehall. After briefing Alec Brown and Richard Brooks, Richard and I went to the urgently convened meeting to ascertain and discuss the details of the requirement. All relevant departments were represented including uniformed senior Navy and Royal Marine officers, senior civilian policy makers and finance officers from GF – altogether there were about a dozen of us. Basically the action fell to Richard and I and we were instructed to drop all other work and to concentrate on the matter at hand. We were tasked to seek offers from the trade for a suitable replacement vessel. Having received a finalised list of basic requirements provided by DG Ships, the technical authority, in consultation with the main players, I referred a request to Reginald Bolton at the Baltic Exchange. The requirement was classed as urgent and in very little time several offers were received from the Baltic Exchange and passed to DG Ships for technical evaluation especially for service in the seas of the South Atlantic. From the offers received the preferred vessel was the Norwegian built, owned and registered cruise ship *MV Polar Circ*le. It was a brand new vessel which had a grand piano and was fully carpeted throughout. It was then declared, subject to certain modification, suitable for service in the Royal Navy. The Charter Party (contract) stipulating the hire period and including the option to purchase the vessel at the cost of £20m was signed. Modification work including extension to the ship's bridge and mobilisation took place at Portsmouth Naval Base and after eight months on hire as HMS *Polar Circle*, the ship was purchased under the option to buy and renamed HMS *Endurance* in 1991.

Whilst the vessel was on hire, Andrew Fricker the new HEO joined and he was given the unusual job of going to the Director of Accounts offices in Liverpool to collect the cheque for the sum of £20m, and travelling to London to sleep overnight in a hotel with the cheque under his pillow. Our Director of Contracts, Alan Banwell presented the cheque to the then owners of *Polar Circle* in a much publicised ceremony in London.

Ex MV Polar Circle. Later to become HMS Endurance

Some years later when working for another department I had the opportunity to go on-board the vessel at Mare Harbour during one of my visits to the Falkland Islands. The ship's personnel were interested to learn how the vessel became part of the RN fleet and I became quite a celebrity whilst on-board. I am only 5'7' and was dwarfed by the royal marine commandos who together with on-board crew invited me to the wardroom for eats and drinks. I was picked up by military vehicle and returned to base a little worse for wear but well enough to enjoy my time on-board the vessel.

Market Testing

Sad though it was, Richard Brooks and I left Andrew Fricker and Dick Westcombe in the chartering section and with my substantive promotion to HEO we became the original members of an entirely new contracts branch set up to administer the Navy Market Testing programme. This was initiated by William Waldegrave, Duchy of Lancaster's White Paper on 'Competing for Quality': I had been told I had been purposely selected because of my background and experience working on contracts in my previous job.

Although not stated in black and white it was soon to be realised as a way of cutting public expenditure by transferring work from certain government departments to the private sector. Civil Service Unions were up in arms and affected staff was seriously worried about their future as it was considered in order to be successful in competition, contractors would reduce staff levels and lower the terms of employment that prevailed in the Civil Service to benefit themselves in a competitive environment.

Richard and I quickly built up a repartee with management

departments responsible for the naval projects that had been selected for market testing. We also gathered together with the help of the Ministry's Central Contracts Policy Branch all relevant documentation pertaining to market testing, many of which were still at the draft form yet to be sanctioned by the unions.

We concentrated our efforts on the first naval project that had been selected for market testing namely the Sandquay Facility operation at Britannia Royal Naval College (BRNC) at Dartmouth The requirement covered the operation of the Sandquay facility site attached to the college by servicing training craft and providing boat repair and maintenance work on all of the BRNC boats which included picket boats, motor whalers and various sailing craft which was operated by the BRNC from the shores of the River Dart. For BRNC to produce an output-based Schedule of Requirements and formulate their own in-house bid was an entirely new concept for the college. As there was scope for the contractor to undertake commercial work, one particular clause Richard added to the requirement was as the crane used to lift vessels in and out the water was owned by the Ministry the successful contractor would pay the Ministry ten per cent of the cost the contractor charged the commercial customer for use of the crane.

I produced the Invitation to Tender document with all the relevant terms and conditions of contract and with Richard's approval the comprehensive invitation to tender was issued to all prospective commercial companies, who had responded to our advertisement placed in the European Community Official Journal, and to the BRNC. The commercial bids were compared to the in-house bid submitted by BRNC in order to establish the most cost effective and technically compliant bid offering best value for money. The contract was awarded to a major facilities management company. The Navy Market Testing Contracts Branch had completed its first project.

Shortly after the award of the Sandquay contract it was announced that all future market testing requirements should cease forthwith until the full implications of TUPE 81, Transfer of Undertakings (Protection of Employment) had been established. Apparently, the reason was that someone thought to be a union worker had uncovered certain information from an EC regulation that had not otherwise been known that could affect and have repercussions relating to the TUPE 81 conditions that Ministry contracts staff had been instructed to adopt for market testing requirements. TUPE 81 was introduced to comply with the EC rules governing the transfer of an undertaking, or part of, from one entity to another. To investigate the issue, meetings were arranged between the Ministry's Central Contracts Policy Branch, officials from the European Community, representatives from the Confederation of British Industry and trade unions, and involved extensive work by the Treasury Solicitor.

This bombshell came out of the blue and, as far as Richard and I were concerned, delayed the issue of invitations to tender for the market testing of marine services, which by then was approaching the final stages of preparation. This project covered the duties and responsibilities of the Director of Marine Services Department with its headquarters at Ensleigh.

The department's responsibilities included the operations of the port auxiliary services at each HM Naval Base covering tugs, passenger movements, moorings, steeplejacks, upkeep and deployment of buoys and salvage equipment at the various salvage depots throughout the UK and certain undertakings of a classified nature. Although we had the availability of a recently retired Commander RN, ex-assistant director and current staff from the Marine Services department to call on for advice as to the operation of the department, we could not rely entirely on the information offered as it would be possible, whether unknowingly or otherwise, that certain information could be held back that could be advantageous to the department when it came to preparing and submitting the in-house bid. We had to ensure we had a level playing field on which outside contractor(s) and Marine services department could base their competitive bids. Accordingly, and as there was little in-house expertise with affordable time available to develop an output-based technical Schedule of Requirements, we placed a contract with an independent firm of consultants to fulfil this task.

With the announcement of the stoppage, this nevertheless did not mean we sat back on our laurels. There were other projects which occupied our time and we progressed many as far as we could up to the point of still awaiting the outcome of the TUPE 81 investigation.

After many months of waiting, eventually the full implications of TUPE 81 were recognised and revised terms and conditions of contract were finally agreed and guidance issued for inclusion in the invitations to tender. The ban was lifted. The outcome in general terms was that, by law, TUPE 81 basically meant contracts of employment must be transferred in total, meaning all individuals' terms and conditions of employment had to remain the same, ranging from pension rights to holiday entitlements and everything in-between, when the whole or part of an undertaking was transferred from one entity to another. In short, commercial bids had to be based on the same terms and conditions as applied to existing Ministry staff including pay and pensions. This safeguarded the employee and ensured a level playing field in competition. As part of the tender evaluation process all bidders were instructed to submit their workers' pension proposals to the Government Actuary for comparison purposes to ensure that pensions were unchanged. The provisions of TUPE 81 were subsequently further revised in later years to accord with the implementation of the European Union Business Transfer Directive.

The market test of marine services took Richard and me (sometimes with the small team of consultants) all over the country, including meetings with the International Chamber of Shipping, UK Chamber of Shipping, Trinity House (Lighthouses), all DMS stations on the Clyde and the Forth, Faslane, Pembroke Dock and Portsmouth, Devonport and Rosyth Naval Bases and PJHQ Northwood. During these visits we met and discussed the market test with representatives of the various unions. Midway through these visits Bruce Amery became our new Assistant Director. Bruce joined us from London and lived in Taunton: he commuted each day mainly by train. Brian quickly familiarised himself with the project and took an active role, and accompanied Richard and me on some of our visits. This was the time when we were spending more time away on duty than we were in office. As it happened this was a good thing as we were moved to an empty office in the Annex to B Block at Foxhill with leaky roof, loose flooring and little heating, on a temporary basis while extra office space was found elsewhere.

There were a number of new projects added to the Navy Market Testing programme and it was not long before it was realised that more staff would be required to cope with the extra demand placed on the team. Soon after Bruce's arrival, new appointees Rona Fairburn and Lucy Manning joined the team. Rona had a background in Human Resources and Lucy had previous 'contracts' experience. Richard and I had built up a good basic record of documentation required for market testing purposes which the new members of staff had access to, so they were able to hit the ground running rather than having to painstakingly start from fresh with a blank sheet of paper.

Being away from the office so much, each member of the team was issued with mobile phones, which were checked regularly to ensure all calls were official and not personal ones – were we to be trusted!?. The market test team was eventually moved to more comfortable accommodation at Ensleigh.

Our Director of Contracts at the time was Alan Banwell who, among other remits, had overall responsibility for the Navy Market Testing Programme and was invited to The Brewery in London along with his opposite numbers from the Army and Royal Air Force departments, who had similar roles, to give a presentation to government Ministers including William Waldegrave, senior civil and service personnel and top executives from commerce and industry. Many companies felt they were in with a shout when certain work was put out to tender and competing with in-house bids. Nathan Easterby was Alan Banwell's staff officer.

After spending a day or so beforehand with Alan rehearsing his speech, with Nathan operating the slide show with a remote control at precise moments to accord with the script and with Richard and me interjecting from time to time with suggested changes, all four of us travelled to London by train for the next day's presentation. Further rehearsals took place in the evening under the supervision of the event's manager and we retired to our hotel. The next day Richard and I were at the back of the hall with Nathan who was given a remote control to operate the carousel of slides. An audience of several hundred filled the hall to the brim. After an introductory speech by William Waldegrave with general slides being displayed onto a large screen above the stage, it soon became Alan's turn, representing the senior service. Following domestic arrangements being explained for the venue Alan was called forward and introduced by the previous speaker and on reaching the lectern handed over his block of slides to the event manager, who installed them into the carousel, and began his presentation. Everything was going swimmingly well with Nathan switching slides in time with the script until a third of the way through the presentation when things went haywire. Unbeknown to Alan and the rest of us, the weight of the pages, which he had been turning over one by one, automatically activated a button on the side of the lectern and the slides began to move randomly at a fast rate forwards and backwards. This continued for about thirty seconds before the manager discovered what the cause was and quickly rectified the situation. He apologised profusely to Alan for not pointing out this particular button beforehand, explaining that if any speaker wanted to override his slide operator it could be done by the press of the button. This caused great embarrassment to Alan but when the cause was rectified he received a sympathetic round of applause from the audience as he recommenced his presentation. Further presentations were given by the Army and Royal Air Force departments and were followed by a question and answer session and, after a few well deserved pints, we returned to Bath by train.

With the TUPE 81 issues now resolved, the invitation to tender was complete except for the pricing arrangement. Badly timed as far as I was concerned, Richard retired and soon afterwards Bruce took early retirement. This left me to devise a pricing arrangement to put to senior management for consideration. No sooner had I completed the proposed method for pricing the requirements, than a new Assistant Director (AD), Godfrey Tonkins, the replacement for Bruce Amery, and David Bainbridge, the SEO replacement for Richard, were appointed. The new AD had arrived a few days before Bainbridge, and I left my pricing proposal with him. David Bainbridge was a fairly young Scotsman of few words and we sat opposite each other in a small office with hardly a word passing between us. As he did not ask to be briefed I became suspicious of his intended plans. I noticed he was reading through my proposal which no doubt had been given to him by Godfrey Tonkins without a word to me. Within a period of a few days, Bainbridge had rewritten the pricing arrangement, and again without a word to me, had obtained the AD's agreement to his rewrite. This really riled me, especially as I had been kept out of the picture and not even consulted over my pricing proposal. I decided that I could not work with these persons and requested an immediate transfer to another branch. I did have some previous dealings with Godfrey Tonkins when he was working in Mat Co-ord and I worked in Weapons finance in the mid-70s and, as far as I recall, the working relationship was amicable.

This was the first time in the whole of my career that I came across a situation like this. Our paths never crossed again. Apparently after the contract was let I was informed problems were experienced relating to the pricing arrangement.

Food (2nd Spell)

Despite the circumstances surrounding my departure from market testing I was happy to return to food supply for a second time in mid-June 1996 albeit with different roles and responsibilities.

My main duties covered contractual management of the existing food supply contract with NAAFI which was now nearing its final stages leading to the point of termination. Besides numerous visits to NAAFI's HQ at Amesbury, my work took me to the Falkland and Ascension Islands and Belize and Germany.

My other duties entailed responsibility for the procurement of food required for in-flight meals and stand-alone contracts placed with contractors on the Falkland Islands and food supply to military personnel servicing at the British Army Training Unit in Belize (BATSUB). I was also responsible for the management of a contract placed with a Monaco based company for the supply of fresh produce to RFA Fort Grange stationed near Split. This was in support of UK peacekeeping forces during the Balkans War (Operation PALATINE). The original contract was placed by someone working in the field who I am afraid was not entirely conversant with food supply. The contract was passed to my section to administer. I found that it was quite loose in terms of detail. I discovered that the contractor was delivering foodstuffs at a whim without any formal instruction or authority for payment. In association with the contractor, I revised the contract incorporating relevant terms and conditions that were mutually acceptable to both parties. This necessitated several visits by directors of the company to Ensleigh to finalise what was now a robust contract.

The Contracts Branch had now been bedded in with members of the Army, Royal Navy and Royal Air Force forming a centralised tri-service organisation namely the Defence Catering Group.

The Contracts Branch was staffed by Sheila Price (SEO), Rodney Munday (HEO), Aden Holder (EO), COs Barry Alpin and Evelyn Evason and myself at EO level. I did not have any supporting staff. Sheila and Rodney were busy producing a competitive tender document to eventually replace the food supply contract awarded to NAAFI some years earlier.

Aden, supported by the two clerical officers, was responsible for the procurement of Operational Ration Packs (ORP) and provisions for the Winter Exercises in Norway by means of competitive tendering adhering to latest European Community and UK Government procurement policies. Aden was quite a character always looking for times to joke but with emphasis on the work side. He would often call out the opening words of the TV programme *Porridge* suitably adapted replacing the name Norman Stanley Fletcher with my name, reciting, 'Royston John Tucker, you have pleaded guilty to the charges brought by this court and it is my duty to pass sentence. You are a habitual criminal who accepts arrest as an occupational hazard and presumably accepts imprisonment in the same casual manner. We therefore feel constrained to commit you to the maximum term allowed for these offences, you will go to prison for five years.' Another of his narrations was often addressed to his clerical officer Barry Alpin which went, 'No man's an island except Barry Alpin', referring to Barry Island in South Wales. Barry was a conscientious worker with a good working relationship with Evelyn. They fully supported Aden and together made an excellent team.

Sheila was generally of good nature but could be a little annoying at times especially when we were confronted with heavy workloads and did not have time to spend on unimportant things. At times it was necessary for me and others to put forward draft letters, memorandums, minutes, etc. for her approval. She was of the mind that although such drafts were word perfect she had to stamp her authority by making silly amendments that had no bearing on the sense, grammar or otherwise of the original draft. It was amending for the sake of it. I did keep copies of her amended drafts as it was evident that some alterations had been changed using the same wording as early original drafts. I felt at times like including examples of both amended versions requesting that she delete as appropriate. I never did but on reflection I wish I had as she may have reflected on how annoying this was as we should have spent our time more effectively. One document I shall remember for the rest of my days was the covering acceptance letter awarding a contract to a food supply contractor. The opening sentence covered sixteen lines of A4 size paper punctuated only by commas, colons and semi colons. Not allowing the reader time to gasp for air. If one of her staff put forward such a draft it would have been rejected outright.

Another annoying instance was when she was on leave. A minute from the Legal Adviser (LA) was received in response to a minute she had written. Rather than waiting for her return I looked at the file and established that her minute to the LA had been written verbatim following a question from the technical department so I referred a copy of the LA's reply onto the technical department for information and any comments, leaving the file in her tray. On her return I thought I was to receive a thankyou but quite the opposite; I received a telling off saying that I should have left LA's minute for her to deal with.

Things did not improve when I was approached and challenged as to why I did not use the MOD hired car system when I visited NAAFI at Amesbury. I always travelled by train and bus. The MOD Bath operated a car hire arrangement for staff travelling on official duty. This less costly arrangement replaced the previous method whereby civil servants could use their own vehicles and claim costs on a mileage basis. I did have my own car but only used it to travel to and from work and in and around the Bath area. Unknown to everyone, except family members and close friends, I became very nervous travelling elsewhere by car because of the trauma I suffered resulting from my accident in 1961. There were no rules to state that staff could not use public transport. To be questioned about this left me embarrassed; however, I stood my ground, advising that, if the department insisted that I use a hired car, I would refuse. My fellow colleagues felt the questioning was trivial and petty. I am not the type of person who would abuse the system, in fact quite the opposite, living so close to my place of work I was often back at my desk within the one-hour lunch break. The person who challenged me chose to ignore this. From that point on I had no respect for the person; neither had my fellow workers.

Sheila captained a skittle team in the Admiralty league and was scorer for the men's CS cricket team, both for which her friend Anton Corby played. Sheila was a popular person socially and she took part in a golf handicap competition I organised among fellow colleagues on the council owned approach course not far away from Ensleigh. Unfortunately, the competition which started enthusiastically was abandoned mid way through due to lack of continued support.

Sheila and Rodney, when he was not socialising in the bar of the Hare and Hounds on extended lunch hours, although he did say and emphasised the point that he stayed on in the office after hours to make up the time, were putting together the invitation to tender for the new, all-encompassing, worldwide food supply contract that would eventually replace the current contract held by NAAFI. The history of the NAAFI involvement with food supply to the forces is explained earlier when describing my first stint in food procurement. Things between Sheila and Rodney became strained and against his will he eventually agreed to join the flexi-working hours system which meant his time could be easily monitored.

With the advent of rationalisation within the Ministry of Defence and a number of departmental changes a new department was created for the purpose of forming a combined tri-service directorate for the procurement and supply of food provisions to all ships and submarines and shore establishments of the Royal Navy, Army barracks and training exercises and all Royal Air Force establishments. Further re-organisational changes followed and the department became the Directorate of Services Food Management (DFSM) and later the Headquarters of the Defence Catering Group. The Group was headed by Brigadier James Light, a one-star ranking officer, whose post was a functional one meaning it could be held by equal ranking officers from either service or by a civilian. The Group was staffed by military personnel from the rank of Warrant Officer 1 up to the rank of Lieutenant Colonel and civilians. The Group was divided under six pillars with each having staff with specialised responsibility for particular areas of work, namely Policy, Contracts, Quality Control & Assurance, Finance, Administration & Personnel and Commodity Management. Civilian staff reported to an Assistant Director Nick James and all military personnel reported through their respective senior officers to the Deputy Head, Colonel David Rowlinson and there was always an open door direct to the Brigadier for everyone.

Team Building became the topic of the day. The object being staff could bond. The department organised several events that included a Race Day at Bath Racecourse and a visit to the Battlefield in France, all free of charge paid for out of the department's budget. Personally, I thought this to be a complete waste of time and money.

I shall always be grateful to Lt Col Mark Maxfield for providing a good insight into Army life and the time spent in answering my questions relating to food supply to the military. Col Max was ably supported by Warrant Officers 1, Craig Holmes and Phil Johnson, and I remain thankful for their assistance.

My first visit to the Falkland Islands was in March 1996. I caught the train from Bath Spa Railway Station to Swindon and the Ministry-hired coach on to Brize Norton for the 23:30 RAF Tristar flight to the Falkland Islands stopping at the Ascension Island for a short time to re-fuel. Check-in went smoothly and for some unknown reason I found myself seated at the front section of the aircraft among VIPs with an empty seat next to me. I think there must have been a misunderstanding remembering I wrote on my flight application form my full rank/grade as 'Executive Officer' which was true and this must have been interpreted by the seat allocation officer as being a high ranking position.

Most of the passengers were squaddies, others being a mix of Falklanders, contractors and dignitaries. The flight was alcohol–free; only tea, coffee, water and meals were supplied. After nine hours and being served with refreshments and a hot breakfast we landed at Ascension Island and all passengers were told to disembark and we were guided to the 'pen', a fenced off area containing bench seats and a NAAFI shop. It was nine o'clock in the morning and with the temperature hitting the mid-eighties the majority of passengers being squaddies queued at the NAAFI shop to purchase cans of beer and lager which had to be consumed before re-boarding the aircraft. I hate to think how much drink was consumed in the forty-five minute refuelling period. For a small fee passengers could have their passport impressed with the Ascension Islands stamp. We were instructed to re-board the aircraft for the onward flight to the Falkland Islands.

The journey down to the Falkland Islands was uneventful until we were about thirty minutes from landing. To our surprise the captain informed passengers that the Tristar had been joined by two tornado aircraft to escort us into Mount Pleasant Airfield. I happened to be in an ideal position next to a window and took the photographs shown on the following pages. The tornado pilots entertained us giving a display on manoeuvrability by playing cat and mouse with the Tristar, flying underneath the Tristar, exchanging positions and flying upright to almost the point of stalling before racing back to sit on the wings of the Tristar.

Photograph taken by Royston Tucker from RAF Tristar being escorted to the Falkland Islands by RAF Tornado, 1996.

Photograph taken by Royston Tucker from RAF Tristar being escorted to the Falkland Islands by RAF Tornado, 1996.

On landing at Mount Pleasant Airfield (MPA) on East Falkland, all passengers, with the exception of the squaddies, before going to baggage collection were escorted into a large room. Here we were given a lecture by the military personnel warning us of the importance of, and shown samples of, land mines, grenades and other munitions and told to report any sightings to the military or local constabulary. The lecture lasted about thirty minutes and we then collected our luggage and passed through security and passport control before in my case being collected by Colin, a member of Civ Sec staff and taken to the accommodation block for senior officers. I was shown the general whereabouts of the senior officers' mess and bar, swimming pool, gymnasium, NAAFI shops and other points of interest and was left to unpack.

The accommodation was very basic; a single bed, very thin mattress and bedding, sink, toilet and a wardrobe. Showers were communal and used by both males and females. Before entry males and females had to ensure there was no one of the opposite sex in the shower area. Occupation was identified by an arrow pointing to male and female signs. I was surprised to learn that the MPA complex main corridor was half a mile long and is the longest in the world. It links the barracks, accommodation, messes, shops and recreation and leisure areas. It was obvious that the weather played a big part in the design of the complex as everything was undercover.

Once unpacked and showered I had a quick tour round before going for my evening meal in the senior officers' mess. A golf course was nearby and I was not surprised to see no one on the course given the changeable weather conditions outside. One minute it was bright and sunny, another it was raining and other times, sleet and snow. Just to see the shredded flags on the greens was enough to dissuade anyone playing a round of golf unless they were well kitted out and prepared to brave the elements. The three course meal was self service with a wide choice of food, cooked professionally by military chefs and followed by cheese and biscuits and coffee. The only criticism I and many others had was that something like cinnamon was added to the milk to prolong its life.

I then walked off my dinner prior to entering the senior officers' bar by means of the combination on the door given to me earlier by Colin. The bar was run by staff from St Helena and Tristan Da Cunha employed by NAAFI. Sitting at the end of the bar enjoying a can of lager, three Gurkha officers came and stood by me and after a short time we introduced ourselves and commenced in general conversation. The Gurkhas told me that they arrived six weeks previous and were on a training exercise. Without any prompting they advised me that they had all fought in the Falklands campaign in 1982 as ordinary soldiers and the stories they told were surprisingly open but frightening in terms of face to face confrontation with the enemy. They were not specific but I understood their drift.

I was later introduced to the Falkland Islands Rations Officer (FIRO), an RAF Squadron Leader and although I had pre-warned him of my visit we discussed my aims for the visit in greater detail. As there was very little else to do I spent the evenings in the bar reading old newspapers and magazines as well as having a few cans of lager to the point of boredom. During these evenings the bar was frequented by RAF pilots which including a female and other RAF, Army and RN personnel, civil servants and commercial contractors. Normally, I would expect most people to drink beer and lager and perhaps white wine for the ladies but as there was no draught drinks, only canned, the common drink was Chilean red wine. I would have liked to know what a night's takings came to!

My main aim of this visit was to put in place a formal contract with Stanley Growers Ltd who were presently supplying fresh fruit and vegetables grown under hydroponic conditions to MPA to afford the Ministry valuable limited cargo space on the twice weekly (Wednesdays and Sundays) UK/FI airbridge for other important and essential supplies. This present arrangement with Stanley Growers had no contractual or financial control and was not in keeping with Government policy and I was asked to formalise the requirement. My discussions with the Falkland Island's desk at the Commonwealth and Foreign Office supported this effort saying that the department should be seen to do everything possible towards the Islands' local economy. As fresh produce supplied by Stanley Growers was to supplement the produce supplied from the UK via the RAF airbridge its capacity was such that it was unable to supply MPA with its total feeding requirement for over 1,000 military personnel and some several hundred contractors, civil servants and visiting dignitary. Stanley Growers' enterprise was also limited in terms of seasonality and product range and therefore the airbridge operation was essential. Food other than fresh produce, was sent by sea from the UK, a voyage of 30 days.

Some years earlier I bumped into Mrs Chadwin, the mother of a friend I knew at junior school who I had not seen since our teens. I can remember her saying her son Eric had moved to the Falkland Islands and went into sheep farming on West Falkland. Recalling this conversation I called to see Mrs Chadwin and explained that I would be visiting the Falklands soon and if she had anything for her son I would be more than happy to take it with me. I later called and picked up a package containing a set of cutlery.

There are numerous islands forming the Falklands but there are two main islands; West Falkland and East Falkland which contains the capital, Port Stanley and the MPA complex.

The second day, travelling by Land Rover driven by Colin I was taken into Port Stanley some thirty miles away to a prearranged meeting with Tim Miller, the owner of Stanley Growers Ltd. En route Colin pointed out Mount Kent, Two Sisters, Mount Harriet, Mount Longdon, Tumbledown Mountain and Wireless Ridge and other landmarks that had seen action during the conflict with Argentina. The road into Stanley was little more than a two way raised dirt road containing lots of potholes with ditches both sides. The landscape was mostly made up of large boulders interspersed with fenced grazing land. Speed had to be kept to a minimum. This land was commonly known as 'the Camp' and is the term used in the Falkland Islands to refer to any part of the islands outside the islands' only significant town, Stanley. The Camp contains various small settlements such as Fitzroy, Fox Bay, Goose Green, Darwin and Port Howard.

There were the occasional floral tributes on the side of the road depicting a death when drivers had lost control of their vehicles and crashed into the ditch. Reaching Port Stanley I first dropped off the package I had brought with me for Eric at the local post office, who by then had married a local girl and set up their own knitwear business on West Falkland. I then paid a courtesy visit to the FI Government offices to introduce myself and to explain the reason for my visit.

We arrived at Tim Miller's market garden which was situated on the outskirts of Stanley on the gradual slopes leading down to the sea, a really beautiful position to admire. Colin said he had business to attend to in Stanley and we agreed a pick up time. Tim showed me round and explained that hydroponics is a method of cultivation of plants in a nutrient rich solution, rather than in soil, and under controlled conditions of light, temperature and humidity. Tim had a number of large poly-tunnel greenhouses containing peppers, tomatoes, lettuce, cucumber and other items of fruit and vegetables at various stages of growth and was ably assisted by his wife Jan and two local workers. Stanley Growers also supplied to the local community. We returned to Tim's house and over a cup of tea and biscuits we negotiated and agreed a formal priced contractual arrangement known as a 'Running Contract' for the coming year. This arrangement is not an actual contract but a vehicle by which orders are placed on an individual basis under the umbrella of the running contract. Each order represents a contract.

Tim also supplied the local community with his produce.

We also discussed Tim's future plans for expansion by growing additional types of fruits and vegetables and the possible importation of fresh produce from Chile. After saying our farewells Colin was there at the agreed time and we returned to Mount Pleasant Complex, but not before calling on a farmer at San Carlos. The purpose of the visit was for Colin to assess claims for damage to fencing, etc. and animal deaths supposedly caused by RAF jets flying overhead leading to sheep and cattle stampeding. I am told that some claims for damage were extortionate and when viewed the damages had little resemblance to actual damage sustained. I was surprised about this as the military was there for good reason.

Although there were recreational facilities available at MPA, these were mainly used by the military to maintain their fitness levels. As far as I was aware staff such as those who worked in the CivSec offices and whose appointments were for a six month period seldom used the facilities and spent a lot of their free time socialising in the bars. In some cases it was evident that civilian staff had to be careful that drink did not get the better of them and should drink only in moderation. Those who did not heed to this found themselves dependent on this way of life on returning to the UK.

The next day I briefed FIRO and went over the workings of the running contract explaining his responsibilities and those of the contractor although this was clearly detailed in the contract document.

I took up Colin's offer to take me to Bertha's Beach to see the penguins. On reaching the beach we walked for about thirty minutes before coming across a rockery of Gentoo penguins. There were literally thousands of penguins on the waters' edge and on nearby grasslands. Colin recommended that we should always avoid standing downwind of the penguins otherwise the smell was not good. It was a sight to be remembered as they huddled together to protect their young. Standing looking south the thought came across me that there was really nothing, except South Georgia and the Sandwich Islands, between me and the South Pole – a weird thought!

The beach was beautiful with its white pristine sand and spectacular waves. I was told that local Falklanders often held barbeques on the beach on Christmas Day.

Unknown to me at the time this was to be the first of a number of visits I made to the Falkland and Ascension Islands.

In addition to using the airbridge for items of frozen and short life food, the Ministry sent other foodstuff by sea from Marchwood Military Port, a voyage taking thirty days.

Space on-board the airbridge was always at a premium and the military personnel in my department were reluctant to give up any of its nominated space for other items of stores in case they lost the space forever. It was accepted without question that food, particularly fresh produce went a long way towards maintaining service personnel's moral.

I made several further visits to the South Atlantic. My penultimate visit was in March 2002 when I was accompanied by Raymond Hammett, the Ministry's Chief Food Inspector.

Following the usual pattern travelling by train and coach to Brize Norton and after checking in for the 23:30 flight to the Falkland Islands via Ascension Island we along with other passengers were directed to the departure lounge. After a prolonged wait we were informed that the Tristar aircraft had a technical fault and the flight would be delayed by one hour. Several other delaying announcements were made before finally being told to go to the canteen for refreshments and then to the Gateway facility for overnight accommodation as there were continuing problems with the aircraft. All passengers were instructed to report back at 7.30 am the following morning for revised departure at 9 am. The Tristar took off on time and we landed at the Ascension Island and went as usual to the pen while the aircraft re-fuelled. This was taking more time than usual and we were eventually told that the aircraft was in need of a replacement navigational probe which would be supplied the next day from the UK. Accordingly all passengers were advised to collect their cabin luggage from the aircraft and we were then bussed to the purposely built accommodation blocks on Travellers Hill for overnight stay.

We were now running two days behind schedule and a number of passengers were concerned about arrangements they had agreed with their contacts on the Falklands and were busy trying to re-arrange their schedules. We eventually arrived at MPA and quickly arranged a revised but shortened programme. We were taken to Stanley Growers by a member of the CivSec staff and Tim gave Raymond a tour of his hydroponic facilities explaining in detail the advantages of using the system in adverse weather conditions. Raymond was impressed with the operation and pleased with the quality of produce. We then went to Tim's cold store to inspect imported Chilean produce which had recently been received by sea. Although the produce appeared to be of good quality however, discussions revealed that the consignment had been sent on a vessel with live animals and had not been properly segregated. It was agreed that Tim would seek assurances that future consignments would be properly packed and isolated in transit before further consideration was given. We discussed the existing running contract and I agreed firm prices for the following three years. On return to the office I issued a summary of the visit and a formal amendment to the contract incorporating the new prices.

My final visit to the South Atlantic took place in February 2003 and was two-ended. I had been in correspondence with the FIRO and colleagues in my department to investigate the possibility of the Falkland Islands supplying fresh bread to the military on Ascension via the return flights on the airbridge and to progress my proposal to place a contract with a Falkland Island company to provide MPA with locally freshly caught frozen Antarctic Rock Cod.

I arrived on Ascension on 10 February and was taken from Wideawake Airfield to my accommodation in a spacious one bedroomed apartment with adjoining shower facilities at the top of Traveller's Hill, not far from the RAF Swordfish recreational centre, bar and restaurant. The accommodation was up market compared to the emergency overnight facilities on Traveller's Hill. The next day I met and discussed the proposal with the rations officer (squadron leader) and agreed the way ahead.

As I had to wait for the next south bound Tristar from the UK and as the island's attractions were widespread the RAF arranged for me to have a hired car for the length of my stay on the island. I made good use of the hired car and travelled all over the island including Georgetown (the capital), Two Boats Village, Green Mountain and although there were lovely beaches only a few were safe for swimming; the others had dangerous under currents. I saw green turtles coming ashore to lay their eggs on the beaches. This was closely monitored by the conservation programme.

A lot of the landscape was volcanic and I was told NASA used parts of the island to trial their moon buggies. A common sight on Ascension is the wandering around of small herds of donkeys who seem to have the freedom of the island. Although fed by the locals they caused havoc to private gardens and parks. I made a special effort to visit the local supermarket in Georgetown and was surprised with the inferior quality and limited availability of fresh produce to the local community. There was no comparison with the produce received by the rations officer on the island from the UK. Apparently, commercially operated sea- and airfreight to the island was infrequent to sustain the needs of the local population.

Driving up Green Mountain with its tight bends and the road very close to the edge and the sheer drops was an unforgettable experience, nerve racking and frightening. Driving down was even worse; I was in need of a stiff drink when I got back to the safety of the Swordfish bar. Sitting at the bar quietly next to a pillar I heard a familiar voice coming from the other side of the pillar.

Without any hesitation I called and said, 'I recognise that voice.' It was Greg Haywood a chap that was a regular at the Old Crown in Weston Village some ten years earlier. He was working on a long term contract with Morrison Engineers and the Swordfish was one of his favourites haunts. We had a long chat recalling some of the regulars of the Old Crown and after a few more lagers we decided to call it a day and go our separate ways.

I flew on down to the Falklands and discussed the bread proposal in depth to the extent that the FIRO agreed with the proposal but certain other aspects had to be taken into consideration. Basically I set up a programme where these aspects could be further discussed in advance of firming up on the arrangement. I am afraid this proposal was further delayed on the cessation of the FIRO's appointment on the island. As I had work in Port Stanley I was accommodated at the Upland Goose Hotel on the front overlooking Stanley Sound.

Turning to the Atlantic Rock Cod, Sam Harding the owner of the fish company had been supplying MPA with the product for some considerable time on an ad hoc basis. The fish was popular as its texture and taste was very much like the cod that was available from the fish and chip shops in the UK. The company had received its EC certification approval for its processing plant. I placed the contract on my return to the UK. This contract was later extended to include the provision of mussels which was treated as a delicacy on the Falklands and consumed at special dinners in the senior officers' mess.

I made several other visits to the Falkland Islands each with specific tasks of a contractual nature to fulfil. During these visits I was pleased to meet up with my long lost friend Eric and his wife Annette who moved from West to East Falkland with their knitwear business. I went to see them unannounced at their shop; he had not changed over the years except for his hardened facial features which had been weather beaten over the years of sheep farming. It was nice to meet up later at the Upland Goose and discuss our schooldays over a few drinks. He mentioned that he was considering moving back to the UK but I could not see him living in an urban environment after spending most of his life on the wind swept Falklands. I did learn that he moved to either the Shetland or the Orkney Islands which are more akin to the Falklands.

Royston Tucker next to a minefield on the Falkland Islands in1996

The turnover of military appointments in my area of work was such that it often affected the continuity within the Defence Catering organisation. An example of this being when it came to light that NAAFI had been operating a long standing arrangement to supply provisions to the British Armed Forces serving at Price Barracks the headquarters of the British Army Training Support Unit Belize (BATSUB), without any proper control or management or the knowledge of the recently formed MOD centralised catering group. Even by consulting NAAFI headquarters at Amesbury my research could not locate any formal contractual document being in place to cover the feeding requirements for up to 100 residential staff and dependants at BATSUB and the regular through put of six-week duration visits at battalion level each consisting of several hundred personnel. The six weeks including training in jungle warfare and afterwards the soldiers spent time diving and canoeing off St George's Caye which contained accommodation and feeding facilities. This was part of the rest and recuperation programme. Having informed my line management of this problem it was agreed that the arrangement should be investigated and put on a formal footing.

My first visit to Belize took place in February 1998. I was accompanied by Lt Col Daniel Burnett (retd), from Army LAND at Andover, Wing Commander Andrew Downing, Defence Catering Group and Nigel Harris (Senior Food Inspector with the Defence Catering Group). The purpose of the visit was to explore the current arrangement NAAFI operated for the supply of food provisions to the British Army Support Unit, Belize situated in the district of Ladyville. Col Daniel had other duties unassociated with food to fulfil during the visit.

We flew from Heathrow to Houston, Texas and over to Belize the next day. We were met by Major Johnstone, QM to BATSUB and hurriedly went through passport control jumping the queue to the annoyance of other passengers and taken to Price Barracks for briefing and then to meet the OinC to discuss our objectives for the visit. The briefing emphasised that certain parts of Belize were dangerous areas and should be avoided wherever possible and on no account should be visited without being in the company of others. Crime was rife especially among teenagers. Local Belizean TV reports I saw before leaving the UK for Belize gave me an insight into the crime scenes. Crime was usually the results of gang warfare normally involving drugs or family vendettas with victims pictured lying dead or injured next to their bicycles. Bicycle was the common form of transport and firearms and knives were prevalent. Unfortunately life is cheap for many Belizeans and we were pleased that we were taken everywhere by top of the range military Land Rover driven by LeRoy of the Belizean Defence Force (BDF) displaying the BATSUB insignia. The vehicle was given right of way by other road users.

After a foot tour of Price Barracks and lunch we made contact with the NAAFI resident manager Keith Michelmore and the BATSUB's Master Chef and agreed we would meet them at 3 pm the following day. The barracks consisted of hurricane force protected living accommodation, sports fields, kitchens, open air type canteens, offices, workshops, a fleet of assorted vehicles, food storage facilities including refrigerated containers, NAAFI shop and a large swimming pool. A part of the barracks was also used for training the local Belizean Defence Force (BDF). I was surprised to see several two- and three-foot-long grey-bodied iguanas appearing from under the flooring of the accommodation blocks to sun themselves. I was told they were harmless and caused no problems. Not quite so frightening as first seeing the dragons of Borneo on TV in the 1950s.

We were then taken to our pre-booked hotel, The Biltmore Plaza on the Northern Highway some 3 miles from the barracks and the same distance from Belize City. After a shower we changed into our swimming trunks and enjoyed the pool and the ambience of the surroundings as the sun went down. As we had eaten we changed and met at the bar and made do with a few beers and tapas type snack.

Our schedule included a courtesy visit to the British High Commissioner's office in Belmopan, the capital of Belize. Belmopan replaced Belize City as its capital some years after

Belize City was devastated by Hurricane Hattie in 1961.

Unknown to us Col Burnett had brought with him two sets of camouflage Army uniforms for Nigel and me and arranged with the OinC of BATSUB for us to fly over the jungle training areas in the unit's helicopter. Unfortunately, I reluctantly had to decline the invitation as on the morning of our flight I was feeling woozy, probably due to something I had eaten the night before at the hotel and my place was taken by Andrew Downing. On his return Nigel could not stop talking of how much he enjoyed the flight. I think Andrew pulled his rank by telling the pilot not to undertake any sudden or fancy manoeuvres, whether he had previously flown in a helicopter was not revealed.

The next day we were picked up by LeRoy and taken to Belmopan a journey of about 40 miles which, because the poor road conditions kept our speed down to less than 30mph seemed to take forever. LeRoy appeared to be subdued and quiet and it was not until well into the journey that he told us he had that morning lost his favourite dog and we were shocked when he explained the dog had been killed by a crocodile when it strayed too close to the river bank.

On our way we pulled in to be passed by a convoy of official cars travelling at fairly high speed with horns blowing and emblems flying. We were told by LeRoy that the convoy contained the Belizean Prime Minister on his way to office. On arrival at the British High Commissioner's office we received an apology from the secretary to the BHC saying he had been called away on urgent business and in his absence we met his deputy, Juan Herrera and explained the reason for our visit to Belize. In general conversation we mentioned that the UK MOD may at a later date wish to open up the food supply to BATSUB to competition, hopefully to include local Belizean suppliers providing all aspects of product specifications and the associated terms and conditions could be met, without reservation. Mr Herrera suggested the names of three local major suppliers that might be approached. Our meeting lasted for 45 minutes and we made the journey back to Price Barracks. Thoughtful as he was LeRoy purchased some bottles of iced cold water for us for which we repaid him.

We returned to Price Barracks and tried unsuccessfully to locate Keith Michelmore and it was late in the afternoon after the helicopter trip, before he made an appearance. We got the distinct impression that he was under extreme pressure and apologised for his lateness. Keith had only been in post for a very short time having been transferred at short notice from NAFFI's food operation in Kenya and with no apparent handover period was finding things extremely difficult even with the help of his local staff.

After the initial meeting with Keith it became noticeable that without any in depth knowledge of the operation in Belize he would be of very little help to us in understanding the mechanism of food operation in Belize. It was therefore decided that Nigel, being the Senior Food Inspector would undertake a full appraisal of all frozen, chilled and ambient foods and fresh produce stock holdings held at BATSUB. This revealed many out of date products and possible cross contamination due to improper segregation. It was also evident that Keith and the recently appointed Army Master Chef was having difficulty in understanding the paperwork available to them. In the meantime Nigel extended the best-before dates on those products he was able to do so without the risk to human consumption and accordingly issued disposal instructions and recommended that Kevin and the Army chef should prioritise future menus concentrating on using products nearing their expiry dates and to adopt a 'first in last out' principle for controlling the remainder of the stock levels having due regard to best before dates. More importantly it was agreed that I should start to prepare a new contractual arrangement for the supply of food to BATSUB. Looking around the NAAFI shop we came across packages of beef marked with the suppliers name Running W and locally supplied Mennonite chicken.

After an exhausting day involving a lot of travelling we returned to the Biltmore and later met up at the bar. After a few drinks Nigel and I decided to retire to our rooms. Remembering the briefing given by BATSUB on our first day we made our way down the paved pathway through the overhanging tropical plants to our ground floor rooms with only the sound of tree crickets. I thought to myself this would be an ideal place to carryout out a mugging. We said goodnight to each other and entered our rooms and prepared for bed. It was not long before I heard a commotion coming from Nigel's room. I thought had he disturbed a burglar or was he being attacked by an undesirable. The noise lasted for about twenty seconds and stopped as quickly as it had started and everything went quiet and as I was in the state of undress I retired to bed. At breakfast next morning I asked Nigel what had happened in his room last night. He explained he had just got into bed and as he was pulling the sheet up to his neck he opened his eyes and saw a large cockroach walking across the sheet inches away from his nose. With that Nigel jumped out of bed grabbing a shoe and chased the cockroach across the floor attempting to kill it. Nigel said he thought he made contact with the cockroach before it disappeared under the wardrobe. I asked whether he had managed to kill it and Nigel replied 'funny enough, when I was leaving the room to come to breakfast the cockroach re-appeared from under the wardrobe with a plaster on its back.' I took this as a joke but whether this was the reason for the commotion I will never know. On our return to the office I included this story in my oral brief to senior staff. I was surprised it never raised even a titter, just the odd groan.

The next day we were taken by BATSUB motor-driven work boat to St George's Caye to see the facilities. On our way we were lucky to see a sea elephant grazing in the shallow waters. The Caye is a perfect place for the military to relax after jungle training. Although basic the accommodation and the Robinson Crusoe-style built straw-and-palm-leaf-covered eating places, pure white sandy beaches and turquoise coloured sea could easily be named Paradise. We were disappointed when the time came to return to the mainland.

During our stay we also visited the Mayan site at Altun Ha to see the ancient pyramids, temples and ruins. We were surprised how well the site was maintained by the Belizean Authority. Altun Ha was occupied by the Mayans for many centuries from about 900 BC to AD 1000 and had a population of about 10,000. Apparently no one actually knows why the Mayans left Altun Ha although it is thought that an intense 200-year drought led to the collapse of the Mayan civilisation. But this is only one theory.

On the way to and from Price Barracks we passed a floral patterned covered building commonly known as the Rose Garden containing a large bar area and girls of ill repute. It was a natural haunt for squaddies to sow their wild oats. Being so close and convenient to Price Barracks I was surprised that this was not out of bounds for our squaddies but I was told that the prostitutes were examined regularly by the BATSUB's medical officer to ensure they were free of any diseases.

It was here in 2001 when a drunken brawl took place between the Gurkhas and members of the SAS who had just finished a jungle warfare exercise. Those present at the Rose Garden, which was apparently staging a strip show, were a group of schoolfriends including the 14-year-old son of a wealthy local businessman and the 16-year-old son of Said Musa the Prime Minister of Belize. Unsure of the exact circumstances whether it was before or after the fracas the 14-year-old sustained serious life threatening injuries and was flown to Tampa, Florida but died three days later. The case against the Gurkhas was eventually dropped.

We left Belize on 15 February 1998 and with an adjoining flight from Miami we returned to the UK and briefed senior staff.

The conclusion of our findings during this visit determined that there was no approved set procedure in place for administering food supply to BATSU Belize and doubt existed as to its financial control and the requirement was in need of a robust contractual arrangement. In the meantime the Wing Commander's cell was instructed to liaise regularly with BATSUB's Master Chef and for Nigel to overcome any foreseeable problems until such contractual arrangement was in place.

After several months of meetings with NAAFI International at Ensleigh and Amesbury, with several other jobs having to take priority I finally agreed and signed a mutually acceptable contractual arrangement with NAAFI for Food Supply to BATSUB 24 February 1999. The contract period of operation being three years, with options to extend, from 1 March 1999 to 28 February 2002 and with firm prices agreed for all products except fresh produce for year one and thereafter subject to annual reviews and firm prices accepted for fresh produce for the initial first month and thereafter subject to monthly price reviews. The Schedule of Requirements contained a total product range of over 200 individual line items.

On 24 February 1999 I placed an Enabling Arrangement with NAAFI International Division at Amesbury to cover the management and supply of food to the British Army Training Support Unit, Belize. Individual orders to be placed under the umbrella of the main contractual arrangement by the BATSUB's Catering Officer the nominated Demanding Authority in conjunction the resident NAAFI Manager whose responsibilities also included replenishment and management of stock levels ensuring that stock turnover is maximised at all times to minimise product disposal.

With the contractual arrangement now reaching the end of its first annual period Simon Chippendale, Senior Food Inspector and I visited Belize in the February of 2000. We stayed at the Ramada Princess Hotel close to the cruise terminal. The main reason for the visit was to check on the effects of the newly introduced enabling arrangement placed in February 1999 and to make tentative enquires with the three suppliers which were suggested by the Deputy High Commissioner as possible sources of supply for future competition.

Our discussions with the Master Chef and Keith the NAAFI manager found that the enabling arrangement was operating satisfactorily and there was no reason for change. We made contact and met with the three companies one of which was the main supermarket operative in Belize City and each expressed an interest in participating in any future competition but indicated that difficulties may rest in meeting our specifications. On our return to Miami we arranged to meet NAAFI's local Miami based contractor who provided certain products including meats. He took us to CISCO's and several other suppliers in and around Miami. Such meetings met with Simons approval.

My third visit to Belize included Nigel and Phil Johnson, an Army Wararant Officer Grade 1 and was a follow up to the earlier visit by Simon Chippendale and which set out the ground work to assess whether the food supply arrangement to BATSUB could be open to competition. We revisited each of the three supermarkets, who had now received copies of a typical draft Invitation to Tender containing Schedule of Requirements, Terms and Conditions of Contract and all relevant product specifications I sent from the UK, who could possibly compete in competition with NAAFI. We also visited Running W cattle farm and a chicken farm operated by the Mennonites.

During a stroll around the cruise terminal we noticed a long queue of nearly a hundred elderly ladies, some on motorised carriages and Zimmer frames, outside the pharmacy. Our enquiries revealed that the ladies were queuing to purchase supplies of Viagra. This was a regular event when cruise ships came into port and the pharmacist had to pay close attention to the cruise ship timetable when ordering replacement stocks of Viagra.

My fourth and final visit to Belize was in February 2003 with Ronald Richards, the recently appointed Assistant Director Grade 6 Civilian, Neil Hind and Phil Johnson. Ronald was the head of the Quality Assurance, Contracts and Finance pillars of the department. He had no 'contracts' background and decided to come along mainly as an observer as I was due to retire in the October. The arrangements for the visit as usual were left to me. We arrived at Miami and as the queues through customs were extremely busy due to the extra precautions introduced following 9/11 we each decided to join separate queues. The mainly Hispanic customs officials were very abrupt and took no back chat. Ronald's queue worked faster than the others and having had his documents processed and stamped he waited close by for the rest of the party to clear customs. He was spotted by an official and told in no uncertain terms to move on or he would be arrested. We eventually all met up at baggage collection and passing without further hindrance we proceeded to board our courtesy bus to the Hilton International Hotel.

We registered at the Hilton and agreed after a shower and shave to meet at the bar. I was first to arrive at the bar and ordered a cold beer and was given a dish of nibbles. No sooner than taking my first sip I felt a tap on the shoulder and as I turned round a voice said, 'is your name Royston?' The person came from the lounge area and was waiting for transport to take him and family members to a cruise ship. I went across and met the family.

Remembering the coincidence involving Greg Harwood on Ascension this was equally surprising as Jean and I had met this family in 1998 when we honeymooned at Club Rockley in Barbados where the family was spending their second week following a cruise. I said that Jean would never believe this meeting and went up to my room on the 17th floor for my camera and took a number of photographs before saying our farewells.

The others by now were waiting at the bar and with Nigel leading we asked the concierge for transport to a popular restaurant on Ocean Drive. A stretch limousine arrived within minutes and we were taken with two other couples who had been waiting to go to Ocean Drive and dropped off outside the Hard Rock Café and told to ask the waiter when we needed transport back to the hotel.

We decided to take a quiet stroll along Ocean View taking in the nightlife and the slow procession of highly polished dream cars and motorcycles stopping at a couple of bars before returning to the Hard Rock Café to eat and back to the Hilton International.

The next day we paid the usual courtesy visit to the British High Commissioner's office in Belmopan. I naturally thought that Ronald being some three grades above mine and more akin to that of the DHC would take the lead but after a few seconds realised that this fell to me. I was not particularly impressed with his attitude and his reluctance to get involved. I think this was also the opinion of the rest of the visiting team.

After completing our first day's schedule and having visited a local Chinese restaurant we returned to our hotel and to the bar. We had been told that the bar was now allowed to serve non-residents. With live music playing in the over-crowded darkened bar, the atmosphere seemed to get tense so we retired to bed after just one drink.

Over the next few days we met with the three Belizean suppliers and visited Running W cattle farm and the Mennonite chicken farm. Each of the three suppliers declined the opportunity to be considered for future competition mainly because of the difficulty in finding suitable suppliers capable of meeting the stringent UK Ministry product specification. It was suggested to the owners of Running W that they may wish to apply for EC approval. Unfortunately the chicken processing plant failed inspection due to hygiene shortcomings. This was reported back to the NAFFI Manager.

To my surprise the return flight to UK was not what I had expected. With Ronald ahead of us at check-n in Miami for our connecting BA flight Phil and Nigel asked whether we could be upgraded as it was my last visit to Belize as part of the Ministry team and that I was soon to retire after 43 years' service in the Ministry of Defence. We were ungraded to first class with flatbeds and champagne, etc., on the upper floor. When we disembarked and informed Ronald he was not a happy man and hardly spoke a word on the car journey back to Bath.

It was decided to extend the existing supply arrangement with NAAFI for further periods as necessary and at a later date consider the requirement for inclusion in the new all-encompassing Invitation to Negotiate Supply, Storage and Distribution of Worldwide Operational and Non-Operational Food, Bottled Water and Catering Disposals which, at the time, was at the draft stage.

CHAPTER TWELVE

COMING TO AN END

Leading up to my retirement I was in regular contact with Personnel Section regarding pension rights, payment and security arrangements and finalising my actual retirement date.

Delegated signing powers had been replaced by the MOD Commercial Licence and my level at the time of retirement was £1m. The licence allowed me to negotiate and sign procurement contracts and amendments to contracts, settlement of prices and to sign price acceptance letters for procurement contracts to the value of £1m. Contracts of higher value had to be referred to a senior officer at the appropriate grade for signature.

The comments made by my countersigning officer on my last annual Performance and Development Staff Report read:

'Roy over the course of the past year has continued to be a dependable and valued member of my team. He is noticeably thorough in his approach to his work and he plans it meticulously. He has produced some very good briefs for me which have been exemplified by his skills as a well organised individual, whose advice is always carefully considered and thus reliable.

Roy has become something of an authority on the contractual aspects of food supply for both the Falkland Islands and Belize. His knowledge and experience will be greatly missed when he retires in October.

Signed

Ronald Richards.'

I was always being told by my superiors that I did not sell myself in front of interview boards. To do so would have been totally out of character for me. I am neither an extrovert nor the kind of person who would put on an act to impress. Many people I knew throughout my career had the 'gift of the gab' and I knew they were no better than I but I could not change into someone I was not or wished to do so. Without being too bombastic I am of the opinion that my failure before interview boards was to the detriment of the Civil Service. After all, why was I successful at one interview and not at others knowing full well that I performed equally well in all my interviews?

I honestly believe that I knew more about the organisation of the MOD than some members of the interviewing board having worked and acquired the appropriate knowledge when I worked in the office of the Director General Ships and maintained an interest in organisational changes that happened since.

CHAPTER THIRTEEN

RETIREMENT

On the occasion of my retirement Jean and I were dined out at the senior officers' mess at RAF Hullavington, the nearest and most convenient military establishment to Bath. We were collected from our house and driven in a staff car, picking up Brigadier James Light and his wife on the way.

On arrival at Hullavington and after attending a pre-dinner drinks reception we were summoned military style by name into the dining hall and directed to the top table, which we shared with Brigadier Light and his wife. There were a mix of Navy, Army and Air Force personnel all wearing service dress uniforms, and my civilian colleagues, about thirty in all, were present.

The evening was a great success starting with prayers, followed by a wonderful five course dinner, toasts and speeches, even the labels on the wine bottles included 'To Commemorate the Retirement of Royston Tucker'. It was a very special and unexpected occasion, masterfully organised by my uniformed colleagues that will stay with Jean and I for the rest of our lives.

I retired on 17 Oct 2003; Jean retired two weeks before me after spending, strangely enough, 43 years as a top 'stitcher' with Clarks, the shoe manufacturers, in Bath.

CHAPTER FOURTEEN

LIFE AFTER RETIREMENT

Shortly after retirement I set myself up as R Tucker Consultancy. This has entailed working for a Monaco-based company, a provider of goods and services to the United Nations (UN) Peacekeeping Missions worldwide, for a Swiss-based company fulfilling requirements for the US Defence Logistics Agency in various parts of the world and to a company also in Monaco serving the cruise ship industry with ambient, chilled, frozen and fresh food and beverages from its warehouses in many ports.

Royston and Jean in retirement

Jean is a volunteer worker in the local Dorothy House Hospice Care Charity Shop in the village and spends hours upon hours doing jigsaw puzzles and adult colouring. In our retirement years we have taken to cruising, our preference being the Caribbean.

Our friends Alistair and Kay Gibson and Babs and Tony Starkey are also keen cruisers and we often cruise together. I play Skittles at the Weston Ex-Services Association and my hobbies include photography, gardening and woodwork.

Up to the age of 50 I must admit I was enjoying the independence of bachelorhood. I left home in 1993 and moved in with Jean, a divorcee whom I had known for several years beforehand. After a week or two I happened to say to Jean, and I wished at the time I had bitten my lips, that she did not iron my shirts as well as my mum. Since then Jean has never ironed a shirt for me. This chore has been left to me and I must admit I have become quite an expert at the ironing board.

God bless.